# WHIPPING UP
# A STORM

Natalie Rowe

domination |dɒmɪˈneɪʃ(ə)n|

noun [ mass noun ]

the exercise of power or influence over someone or something, or the state of being so controlled


dominatrix |ˌdɒmɪˈneɪtrɪks|

noun ( pl. dominatrices |-trɪsiːz| or dominatrixes)

a woman who physically or psychologically dominates her partner in a sadomasochistic encounter; broadly: a dominating woman

# Author's Note

It is important to ensure that the details of some of the individuals encountered through my work are not set out in a manner that would enable people to recognise them. With careful consideration however, I have decided NOT to conceal the identities where I feel it is of public interest and to highlight the hypocrisy of others.

# One

# THE CITY BROKER

"Hello?"

"It's me John"

On the other end of the phone was John, he was calling me from his office. John worked at Lloyds of London, where every day he was handling Millions of people's investments. He was confirming with me our appointment later that day.

"Guess what I'm wearing Mistress?"

"What are you wearing John?"

Imagining a new suit or something

"Mistress I'm wearing a pair of stockings under my trousers"

"You are a naughty boy John"

"Dose it please you?"

"Of course, it does, what made you do that?"

"I have a confession to make"

"What's that John", I said in a curious and stern voice

"They're your stockings Mistress, I hope you don't mind but I took them on my last visit to you"

"That was very naughty of you John"

"I know Mistress, you can punish me when I come over later"

"Why did you take them without my permission?"

"Because I wanted to feel close to my Mistress, and guess what else I've got right here with me?"

"Tell me?"

"The pipe"

At first I was bewildered, it couldn't be ….

"As in the crack pipe?"

"Yes"

"What! You're smoking in the office at work?"

I knew then that John was heading down a slippery slope if he was now smoking crack at work!

"You'll get caught", I whispered down the phone line

"No I won't and anyway, the doors locked"

And sure enough he lit the pipe, while I listened, then he blew the smoke out.

How on earth was he going to function, high on crack, I wondered. He was playing a dangerous game.

"I'm high now Mistress", His voice now sounding different, as the cocaine took a hold.

"I can't wait to see my Goddess and worship at your feet."

I was nervous for him, that he would get caught or someone would smell the odour that the crack was surely giving off.

"Right Mistress, I'll see you later, back to work".

John was a long time regular, he had been a cocaine snorter when I first met him, nothing unusual there, but he had now switched to Crack.

What he told me was that while I'd been on holiday, he had visited another vice girl and she said she couldn't get any to snort and had introduced him to crack cocaine.

A lot of crack addicts prostitutes, were now deliberately introducing the stuff to their clients in order to support their own habit, plus in many cases their pimps were the suppliers.

This was now the Lloyds of London' Executive drug of choice

*

I came from a respectable back ground, and I wanted for nothing. Every Sunday I took piano lessons and one day a week I attended drama school.

I was an athlete, breaking the Yorkshire record for the under 15s even though I was only 13. I was a star netball player, and a popular girl.

An A student in my class, but always felt a bit of an outsider. I loved to sing, grew up listening to Motown, ska, and Northern Soul, I knew all the Marvin Gaye hits and every Sunday morning I would pretend I was singing a duet with him. I was going to be famous, just didn't know when or how.

My parents were born in Jamaica, and emigrated to England, I was born in Bradford, Yorkshire, was one of two children, and had a happy childhood, I was the black sheep in the family, just felt I was destined to do something other than get married have a few kids and go to the Mecca Club on a Saturday night, and have roast chicken and Yorkshire pudding on a Sunday.

The cold cobbled streets and the cotton mills the same familiar chit chat every day, just didn't appeal to me even at that young tender age.

I never felt that I fitted in, I felt too contained, and one day having experienced a loss of a close family member, I ran away, couldn't get to Hollywood - so London would have to do ......

# Two

# A SHELTER

Now a teenage runaway when I arrived at Victoria coach station with 30p and a packet of luncheon meat sandwiches to my name. I already missed my dad and brother desperately but I swore I'd make them proud of me one day. As I left the station I started to marvel at this new and strange city and, a short while later, lost, I decided to take a seat at a bus stop.

An old man came and sat next to me. He made eye contact a couple of times before leaning over and saying 'Hello.'

I looked back at him shyly.

"Busy?"

"Doing what?"

"Looking for business?"

"What do you mean?" I answered, looking confused.

"Sorry. Forget it." He got up and left.

Hours passed. I sat, shivering from the cold, watching commuters. As the rush-hour crowds thinned I forced myself to get up and walk the streets. It started to rain and I was soaked by the time I found shelter in a covered bus stop. Three black guys sat next to me. They were laughing and joking and seemed nice. One of them offered me a cigarette. We started to chat. I told them a bit about myself, shed a few tears, they took pity and took me home with them. The Yorkshire Ripper, Peter Sutcliffe turned out to live next door to one of my neighbours and so the last thing I should be doing was wandering off with 3 strangers, my instincts told me that I could trust these young men. Going off with those three boys isn't something I'd do now, but I'd been talking to them for a while about my life and I could tell from the way they responded that they wanted to do the right thing.

They lived in a house in New Cross, I was so glad to have somewhere safe to stay, what would I have done had they not offered to help me. We talked about Yorkshire what it was like there, they cooked me supper and assured me I was welcome to stay for as long as I needed. I'll never forget their kindness.

The following morning one of them showed me an ad for a job as a chambermaid in a hotel. Room and board was included.

Perfect.

*

The Mount Pleasant Hotel was in Kings Cross, a Victorian building on the corner of Calthorpe Street and Kings Cross Road, originally a doss house for working class men. At the interview I said I was 18; the manageress didn't ask for ID and I was paid in cash. My job was to make up the beds and clean rooms all day long.

Nobody ever checked my ID. I was confident and looked old enough, so there was no reason for them to. I even managed to open a bank account under a false name (Natalie Edwards) without using ID, you could in those days, and would take my brown envelope containing £33, my week's wages and pay it in. It was a tidy sum, especially as room and board was covered. Having my own money felt great.

I shared a damp and smelly room with warped floors with two other girls (Lisa and Katrina), a family of cockroaches and a handful of mice, in a house not far from the hotel. We didn't talk much about our backgrounds as we were all running away from something. We were united in our emotional pain, missing families and friends. One dark-haired Scottish girl told me that her father had sexually abused her. On those occasions we did mention our parents, I talked as though mum was still alive.

We all smoked cigarettes – I was still not into alcohol, because of the taste. I stuck to Advocaat (my Xmas drink as a child)

I certainly didn't want to spend any of our free time in our little room, I went with Lisa and Katrina to Park Lane – all I knew was that it was the most expensive section of the Monopoly Board, and that was where I wanted to be.

I was our unelected leader – I couldn't help myself, I was always the boss – and if I wanted to go to see the hotels of Park Lane, then we all did. I always made the decisions about where we were going and when.

We stood outside at first, looking through the windows of the elegant Dorchester and the more modern, skyscraper-style Hilton, at the chandeliers and the cars pulling up, unloading the great and the good. I was the first to walk in for a closer look, followed by my new friends. Even though we clearly didn't fit in, no one stopped us and we explored the luxuriously spacious loos, testing the perfumes and soap, admiring the huge mirrors, fancy lights and patterned tiles. I thought if I ever ended up homeless again, I'd sleep in the toilets of the Park Lane Hilton, a silly thought I know now.

Work at the hotel was long - beginning at dawn - and

dull - remaking bed after bed after bed after bed - but starting early meant we finished at 3.30pm. I spent nearly all my spare time sitting in the lobbies of 5-Star hotels. I breathed in the smells of fresh flowers, expensive perfumes and leather; I eyed the rich and the beautiful calling for porters and chauffeurs, sometimes in foreign languages. This was where I needed to be.

I attracted lots of male glances. I didn't know then what those looks meant; I just thought they were being friendly, it's more likely they thought I was a hooker, waiting to be picked up.

Each night I returned to my shabby room, dreaming about the clothes, jewels and hairstyles of the women I'd seen coming and going, and told myself that I was going to have all that one day, instead of hanging around, I'd be a guest.

I didn't know how soon it was going to happen, but it would.

# Three

# SOHO

One night after work I was reading Girl About Town when I spotted an advert for hostesses in Soho. The pay was £75 per week. I wasn't sure what a hostess was exactly, but £75 was a fortune.

The woman who interviewed me was in her late twenties and smoked and squinted at me as she asked her questions, starting with how old I was.

I replied immediately.

"Eighteen."

Even though I was under age, with makeup, and thanks to my height and full figure, I could easily persuade any man I was far older.

The woman nodded and explained that my job was to encourage the gentlemen customers at the club to drink as much as possible. If they bought 'champagne' (a foul and hugely overpriced sparkling wine), I'd earn a commission. The same went for cigarettes. They sold large rectangular boxes of fifty Dunhill, at ridiculous prices; the commission on them was about £12 per box.

"And if you decide to leave with them, they have to buy two bottles to take away."

Leave with them? Why would I leave with them? I had no idea. I just nodded, thinking of the £75 salary.

8

The club's owner was a lively, dark-haired, moustachioed, money-obsessed Irishman with receding hair called Connie – he'd once been a Catholic priest but the Devil had got him good.

He ended up in the News of the World after a journalist exposed his 'dens of vice.' Unfortunately, the journalist had taken pictures of the girls and put them in the paper with price tags pinned to them, showing their individual charges. One of the girls was a 'good' Catholic girl, who hadn't told her family what she was doing. They disowned her after that.

Connie's seedy clip joint was in Greek Street in Soho, a rough area back then, and poorly policed. Young girls stood by doorways, acting as bait, luring in tourists who were then quickly fleeced of all their cash once they got inside.

Being on the inside, everything was exciting to me, as was London itself. Shortly after I started working at Connie's, some of the other girls took me across the river to south London to meet a woman known only as Miss B.

It was night time when the taxi took us over the Albert Bridge, all lit up, sparkling golden light on the Thames. At that moment, I felt as if I'd really 'arrived' in the capital – I was certainly on my way. Miss B turned out to be a female Fagin and if you lived in the underworld as I now did, then you needed to know who she was and pay your respects – or a cut out of whatever criminal enterprise you'd started, mostly to deal with thieving, such as shoplifting or stealing goods from warehouses. Her large house was packed full of ornaments, pay offs from a thousand shoplifting expeditions.

Miss B was a hardcore Jamaican, in that she spoke with such a strong accent it was hard for most people to understand what she was trying to say. She spoke in a gruff voice as she welcomed me. I liked her immediately and she took me under her protection, demonstrated soon afterwards when I had a blazing row with one of her sons, I can't remember what it was about, but we both had short tempers and he ended up slapping me. Miss B was up in a flash and slapped her son in the face, telling him "You don't hit women, no matter what." Even thieves could have a moral code.

Miss B often said to me: "One day you're going to be rich and famous and will forget all about me."

Connie's clip joint had bouncers and, if we didn't like the way a man was behaving, we'd signal them and they'd place a heavy hand on the customer's shoulder and escort them 'elsewhere'.

Issues often arose with tourists who didn't realise they were paying for the girls who came over and started chatting to them – they didn't know they were being 'hosted' – and the cost for three girls quickly mounted up. Once an argument began the men had no hope of winning. No one left without paying. If necessary a couple of the really heavy-duty bouncers would come out – no one dared to call the cops – trying to pick up girls this way was illegal anyway. The client would be escorted to another room, through a side door, and I never found out what happened behind there. Sometimes customers had to leave expensive watches and rings, or their driving license or passport as deposits until they got the cash to pay all the club fees.

I left my chambermaid job as soon as they told me I was hired, and moved to a hostel in Bayswater where, for £2.50 a day, I shared a long room full of beds with six other girls (it's now a high-end, £500-per-day luxury apartment let) I ended up recruiting two girls who'd been working in a shoe shop to come and join me at the club. They were unsure but I said: "Of course you can, it's easy." They both ended up being fully-fledged hookers.

It didn't take long for me to realise that some of the girls slept with their customers for a lot more money. I was too frightened of this at first and I did okay from 'champagne' sales. As a hostess you'd expect to make £20 a night without sleeping with anyone. For sex, you would make £60 or more, which in the late 70s and early 80s was great money.

Not all men wanted to sit with a black girl. Scandinavians, Germans and Belgians tended to request black girls. A lot of black girls went to work in Germany and Belgium at this time (Laura made fortune out in Belgium). I was only put on an English table if the men specifically requested a black girl, or if all the white girls were busy. I was quite angry that the presumption was that English men wouldn't want a black girl.

Foolishly, I kept all my money on me at this time, all made simply through commission from getting the guys to by the crap Champagne and cigarettes and it was stolen from Connie's club. This left me with an urgent problem – no money to pay for my hotel. I needed to make a lot of cash, fast.

# Four

# THE FIRST

The touts did a good job getting 'Mr. Lebanon' inside; he was a cut above the usual clientele: finely cut suit and long cashmere coat, diamond watch, tall, dark and handsome. He arrived with another well-dressed man who turned out to be his assistant.

All the girls' eyes were on him.

The woman in charge came over to me. "He's asked for you."

"Really? He wants me?"

I was flattered but puzzled; he could have chosen any girl out of the twenty or so that were here.

When he asked me to leave with him I agreed, I needed money to pay for the hotel, so it had to be today that I was going to do it with a complete stranger for the first time. We had been sat at the table drinking and chatting general stuff, he kept saying how much he liked me, he'd made me feel at ease. He took me from Connie's to the Westbury, a 5-Star Hotel in Bond Street, on the way in the cab, I was full of excitement not in the least bit nervous. The suite had floor-to-ceiling windows that overlooked the whole of Mayfair. I'd never seen such a huge bed, nor felt such luxurious sheets. A bottle of Crystal Champagne arrived. It was like nothing I'd ever tasted – liquid gold, dancing in my mouth, lemon, peach and sunshine. Mr. Lebanon had ordered two bottles from Connie's but hadn't touched them. Now I knew why.

Although he had a thick Lebanese accent, his English was perfect and he spoke like a gentleman. I seemed to know instinctively what was expected of me: to be charming, to listen and show interest, compliment his looks and charm. I was an actress playing a role; confident yet coy at the right moment. I felt as though I had done it all before. For a moment I wanted to tell him he was my first client but I didn't want to seem unprofessional, so kept quiet, plus he wouldn't have believed me probably.

I went to the bathroom, freshened up, undressed and examined myself in the mirror. My teenage body, young and athletic, was perfect. I took a deep breath and walked back into the bedroom.

He studied me for a moment. "This is for you Natalie," he said, handing me £100. I'd been so caught up with what was happening that I'd completely forgotten that I was supposed to be paid.

"Thank you." I put the cash in my cheap handbag, resolving to get a new designer one at the first opportunity.

We were alone and naked now. I sat next to Mr. Lebanon, conscious of his hairy body and fresh smell. I had a condom in my hand and placed it on the bedside table. He began to stroke my breast and then took my nipple in his mouth. His lips were soft and I began to feel extremely aroused.

The sex was straightforward, short but sweet.

Afterwards I took a shower and dressed, I stayed for another hour, eating whatever he ordered from room service. It had been the most beautiful day in my life – so far and now I had to return to my shitty little world. More than ever I knew I wanted to be a part of the universe Mr. Lebanon's inhabited.

I know now that the experience had felt normal to me because I had control. Nobody had coerced me – I had given myself willingly; in fact I'd used Mr. Lebanon to get what I needed – my rent money. In reality we had struck a deal. Also, now I'd had a taste of luxury, I wanted more.

As I was leaving the hotel, the doorman leaned over and asked: "Taxi madam?"

"Oh, er, yes please."

This was a first. But of course I had the money. He lingered at the door as I got into the black cab, and I guessed, correctly, that he wanted a tip.

Once the driver pulled up outside my hotel I tipped him too. He smiled at me and said: "Be lucky."

# Five

# AND DOWN CAME THE RAIN

I don't know if it came from being around hookers in Connie's, or if I was born with a talent, but whatever skills I had, they were perfect for what I was doing. Now that I understood the game, I played the role to fit.

By choosing me over all the other girls at Connie's, Mr. Lebanon had helped me realise I was hot stuff and therefore turned me into a confident young woman.

Before Mr. Lebanon, I'd just wait at the bar and watch other girls march over and started chatting to potential customers. After Mr Lebanon, the initial fear and embarrassment of rejection had had left me. I discovered it was much easier than I thought. I'd start by asking: "How are you doing, how's your day been, the usual patter" It was very rare I didn't clinch the deal. If they weren't going to have me then they weren't going to have anyone.

It worked. I made £1,000 in just one week and moved to a better hotel. Now, for £20 a day, I had a room with an en-suite, TV, phone and maid service. Conscious of the fact that not too long ago, I too was a maid, so I always left a good tip for room service.

I never liked the word prostitution. To me - and I'm

sure to the vast majority of people - it has negative connotations. It suggests submissively handing your body over to a man who can do what he wants, fag ash Lily on a street corner and that the female has no self-respect.

I prefer the term vice girl – and I had a great time at it, I had the best laughs, sex and experiences. I enjoyed the attention and affection. I had (in some cases) much worse experiences during 'normal' relationships.

There's something sexy about control. I feel great when I've got hold of a man's 'weakness' - when you've got them in that position, they're like vulnerable babies, the one thing they want above all else is to come, so I tease them, making sure I have complete control; they're not going to have an orgasm unless I'm going to give it to them – and so they end up promising me anything until I give them what they want.

I quickly learned how to pace it. I knew how to get any man the most excited he'd ever been, so by the time he exploded it was the best fucking orgasm he'd ever had, the most exciting moment of his life. I really believe I'm the best at this. I'm a giver – and want to give the best I can. In the back of my mind is the idea that I want him to want me and miss me afterwards because he's never going to find anyone better.

I was cold and calculating in that my aim was do what's required and get my reward as quickly as possible. I certainly didn't want to be verbally intimate – to act as if I was a client's girlfriend. I was able to enjoy the experience precisely because it was shallow – I was turned on by the fact that the man wanted me and I could give him more pleasure than he'd dreamed of. Afterwards I was able to walk away and get on with my life. It was liberating and it's an adventure finding out the right buttons to press, and seeing it work. When in a personal relationship it's filled

16

with all the 'what if's', in a strange sexual encounter there's no complications just raw sex.

*

I was making lots of money now, so that meant more shopping in Oxford Street. One day I decided I needed a wig. A shop assistant said Shepherds Market was the place to go. She meant Shepherds Bush Market, not Shepherds Market in Mayfair.

I realised I was in the wrong place just as the cabbie pulled away, leaving me standing in my record-breaking high heels and short pink dress with plunging neckline. As I started walking, I realised I was at the back of Park Lane, I had no idea the area minutes away was called Shepherds Market a notorious spot for working girls.

I noticed girls in doorways, and cars slowing down, girls chatting at car windows. A man in a chauffeur's uniform approached me and asked me if I'd speak to his boss. He said we'd better not hang around otherwise we'd get arrested.

"For what?"

He smiled. "Aren't you working?"

We approached a light blue Rolls Royce with a soft white leather interior. Inside was a very handsome, slim, dark haired, green-eyed, 30-something Italian.

"My name is Francesco. Would you like to join me at my hotel for a drink and something to eat?"

He took out an envelope.

"There's £500 in here, to start. There will be more, depending on how versatile you are."

His hotel was the Londonderry, now the Metropole, next to the Hilton. It was like being in a movie – stepping out of a Rolls Royce into a 5-star hotel, doors being opened for me every step of the way.

Francesco asked me to put on black stockings and suspenders. I got changed in his beautiful ornate bathroom. When I emerged he was naked and his cock was so hard it looked ready to burst.

"I want you to sit on the bed and watch me play with myself. When you think I am about to come, tell me to stop and slap me across the face. Do you understand?"

'Weird,' I thought, but nodded.

He knelt before me and started to masturbate, calling me a black beauty' hmm that name stuck in my mind. He soon started to groan.

"Stop it."

"Slap me, I'm a naughty man."

I hesitated. Was he sure? I slapped him.

"Harder!"

The next time my hand stung.

"I'm sorry Madam." He bent down and started licking my shoes, what's all this about, I thought, this is all a bit weird

"Let me suck the heels madam, please." yep, this guy is odd.

I lifted my foot and gently pushed the heel into his mouth as he sucked and licked, trying not to hurt him and at the same time trying to keep a steady balance. 'Hold on' he said, and a few minutes later after he'd fiddled with the combination on his brief case he fetched another envelope of cash.

"Natalie, if you can do the next thing I ask of you, this is for you."

I eyed the cash. I wanted it, so whatever he needed from me, I was game.

I followed him into the bathroom and he sat in the bath.

"I want you, madam, to urinate all over me. I am bad and deserve it."

I was incredulous. "You want me to wee over you?"

"Yes."

"Okay, if that's what you want, I'll try."

At first I couldn't do it – it was a mental thing,

It wasn't easy, straddling a slippery bath with killer heels. I shut my eyes, tried to relax – it was a question of me getting through that barrier. Then suddenly the monsoon arrived! And once you start, you don't stop, so a golden shower spayed over Francesco's hair, face and across his chest. He ran his tongue over his lips, full of gratitude as if he'd just been rescued from a desert Island.

"Thank you madam, thank you."

Luckily he didn't ask to kiss me afterwards, I would have had to draw the line right there.

As far as Francesco was concerned, I thought he was one weird fucker. Having said that, I left the hotel with a thousand pounds – I was rich! Whatever Francesco needed from me to get off, I was happy to be as versatile as long as the price was right.

To some extent I didn't know what was weird or normal because of my naivety but sometimes there was no mistaking it. Not long after this I ended up with a client who asked me – along with another girl – to put pins through his nipples. The fee for this was several hundred pounds.

"No problem!" I said, "I'll do one you do the other."

The other girl shook her head and retreated to a corner of the room.

"Why can't you do it? He's paying us."

She just shook her head again and whimpered.

I shrugged. "More cash for me then."

Many couldn't do it, but I never had a problem fulfilling a painful request.

Francesco, who was a commercial lawyer, became a

regular. Our sessions would, over the months, then years, become more extreme as he grew to trust me. He flew me out to Rome, Milan and Venice, I would even pick out clothes for his wife while shopping in the beautiful shops sweet Italy had to offer. See what men are like? Wonder how many wives right now are wearing clothes picked out by their husbands Mistress? My guess, a lot! Francesco changed my life; he opened my eyes to the profitable possibilities of working for myself, independent from a seedy joint in Soho - all because of a mix-up over an address.

## Six

# STREET LIFE

After finishing with Francesco that first encounter, his driver dropped me off in the 'real' Shepherds Bush Market – in Shepherds Bush. He gave me Francesco's card and then his as well, "Just in case."

It was something else, being in the back of a Roller on my way to the market, noting the curious glances from pedestrians and other drivers – I felt exhilarated, like a super star. I lapped it up, and wanted the journey to last forever but we arrived soon enough and I climbed out of the Roller, ready to look for my wig.

But, as I watched the car disappear, I had a bit of a panic attack about what had just happened. I felt as though people were staring at me, as if they could tell I was a vice girl, I wasn't exactly dressed to go shopping in a market, should have dressed more appropriately, I looked tarty and having just stepped out of such a fancy car, I felt on show and rather exposed.

Shaking, I forgot about the wig and took a taxi straight back to my hotel. As I shut the door, I was overcome by a wave of nausea. I dropped my bags and ran for the loo where I puked until I thought my stomach would burst. Suddenly, all the tension and fear of what had just happened was released. I was safe in my haven, my little

21

hotel room in in Lancaster gate.

Now I knew where to go if I ever wanted to make a lot of cash – but I wondered if my nerves could take streetwalking, even if it was Park Lane. I thought that as long as I trusted my instincts I'd be okay. Usually, when my back was against the wall, some kind of survival impulse took over.

After a slow night at Connie's, I grabbed my handbag and headed home, but when I looked inside I saw all my cash had gone, AGAIN! I was being targeted I was certain I knew who it was, the thieving bitch, a girl who never did much business in the club and hardly ever left with a client, I complained, and was told that it had happened to a few of the girls recently. I had noticed her a few nights back fumbling in a bag under a table, I had presumed it was hers, now I realised it was probably another girl's bag she was robbing. I was going to keep a good look out for her from now on.

My next week's hotel money was due. I had no choice but to head straight for Park Lane, I kind of wanted to, it was like going on a new adventure, never knowing what was down the road literally

As I crossed the border of Soho and entered Mayfair, I started to feel self-conscious.

'Calm down girl,' I told myself.

I pretended I wasn't a hooker; I was just a girl on my way home. Nevertheless, I noticed more than ever the sharp clicking sound of my heels on the pavement as I crossed Bond Street. I didn't want to be noticed, but how else was I going to make any fucking money?

Park Lane was a different world by night and I felt scared, but there was excitement at the thrill of the unknown too. I saw girls in doorways, cars stopping, girls getting in.

One girl suddenly shouted: "Fuck off!" at a client.

Another got out of a car, her nose bleeding.

I shrank back into the shadows. It was so different in the club, which was indoors and came with protection.

I didn't want to stand near the other girls; so picked less obvious patches to stroll, such as Grosvenor Square. Other girls were in Curzon St and Hereford St just behind Park Lane, as it wasn't as well lit, and that was where I first spotted the meat wagon, (a phrase I picked up from the girls) the police van, doing its rounds. Some cops were paid off by pimps - with cash or sex – to leave us alone.

A car slowed and started to crawl alongside me. I walked on as if I hadn't noticed. He drove a little way ahead and then stopped. My heart was racing. He could take me away and murder me; at least at the club there were witnesses.

Heart pounding, I knelt down to the window.

"Get in."

"A hundred."

"Too much, darling."

"How about fifty?"

He laughed. "You're new, aren't you?"

"Not really."

"Forty to fifty is the going rate. I'll give you sixty for a wank."

"Sixty for a wank?"

"Yes, that's right," he said, still smiling. "A wank."

A five-minute hand job would pay for three days in the hotel. I got into the car, shut the door and we sped off.

"Your place or mine?" I asked thinking of my hotel.

He laughed.

"No sweetheart, we're going to pull up in a bit and we can do business there."

We stopped in a pitch dark, silent mews terrace and he handed me three twenties.

This was a good spot, I felt secluded but lots of nice-looking houses around. 'Probably lots of judges, lawyers and politicians,' I thought, 'If only they knew.' Of course, they probably did, and some of them might be clients.

I felt good. There had been no need for names or niceties. This guy really knew what he wanted.

He leant back, sighed and said: "It's all yours."

"Come on start wanking darling," he snapped impatiently, "I've no time for foreplay."

"Well, if that's what you want."

He stopped me. "Hang on a moment."

To my dismay, he spat on his hand and wiped it all over his bits.

"That's what you do darling," he said, "Get it nice and wet."

I wasn't pleased at all to have to touch his spit – I didn't mind touching his cock at all but I found his spit gross.

As he seemed to be in urgent need, I started - vigorously.

He moaned, tensed, arched his back and fired his ammunition

I had a 'note-to-self' moment as I realised I had nothing in my bag with which to wipe the mess. Luckily he had some wet wipes.

He dropped me off back in Grosvenor Square and sped off without a word. As I watched him go, the same panic I'd felt after my experience with Francesco started to rise. What the fuck was I doing? I had come to London and reinvented myself – but what kind of person was I going to be? I had no idea, although I felt as though these experiences had already changed me forever.

'I'm alive' I told myself, getting a grip, 'nothing bad has happened.'

Making a living this way could be easy, I thought - as

long as I was careful. Before I had time to think, a Mini pulled up alongside me. At least finding clients wasn't going to be difficult, I thought to myself. The song - Bad Girls by Donna Summer, kept ringing in my head.

## Seven

# THE ACTOR

I was braver now I'd turned my first trick and I climbed straight into the Mini.

"Hi, I'm Simon. You're new."

I got in, thinking this was could be another quick hand job in a backstreet.

"Where do we go?"

"My hotel. Don't worry, I've tipped the doorman, he knows what I'm up to."

Tipping, I would soon discover, was vital. Doormen are wonderful allies with fantastic memories. If you didn't tip you wouldn't always get in – unless the client had tipped them in advance – as Simon had in this case. The doormen always knew what I was there for – there weren't many black girls wearing designer dresses a dodgy wig and killer heels staying as guests.

The Hilton's concierge, bellhops and doormen all knew the working girls and helped them do their jobs (which was, after all, keeping their wealthy clients happy). The Ritz and Claridge's also never presented a problem for working girls. They knew what their guests wanted and saw no problem in going beyond the normal call of duty. Lots of money changed hands and a great many 'freebies' were given, but it was all handled with a friendly professionalism. One hooker I knew had a child by a senior executive of one major hotel chain and she was sorted for places to carry on her business after that.

The less-classy establishments were stricter. In fact, the less classy the hotel, the snobbier the staff, I've found. There was a limit to the scope of their service. The staff at the Hilton and The Ritz and alike, had minds so broad you couldn't see the horizon. The Cumberland in Marble Arch on the other hand, wouldn't let me through the door and so the Dutch guest who'd booked me checked out that night in fury and moved to the Hilton, his surname was gold and he certainly lived up to his name.

As Simon drove I asked him what he did for a living.

"I'm an actor, I've been filming a series for the BBC."

"What's it called?"

"Enemy at the Gate. It's a war thing, with lots of action."

We arrived at the hotel, Simon nodded to the concierge who nodded back, and up we went.

"Do you mind cigars?" he asked, as we stepped into the room.

"No." I had no idea; I'd never even smelt a cigar before.

He lit up. The room was small and the smell was very strong. I liked it.

We cuddled and kissed for a while, then Simon took the initiative and I went along with it. He was gentle, first touching my nipples, then my pussy, taking his time. I enjoyed the intimacy, it was something I'd been in short supply of since coming to London, and it turned me on. I barely knew this man but everything he did made me feel wanted and safe.

I was also attracted to his artistic nature, as well as his deep actor's voice. I enjoyed the fact that he talked more –

he wasn't like the man in the sports car, who'd been nothing but business. Simon made what we were doing feel so sophisticated and made me start to see hooking in a new way – he made it into a beautiful occasion.

By the time he penetrated me, as far as I was concerned, we were making love, the fact I was being paid had become incidental. Then he stopped.

"What's wrong?"

"Nothing, I don't want it to end too soon."

We talked for a little while; I told him I wanted to become a singer. A few minutes later he asked politely if he could taste me.

"Okay."

It was lovely; soon that delicious feeling began.

"Oh! I'm going to come."

"So come, if you want."

I held on for a bit longer and then came and it was wonderful. He carried on, until I couldn't take any more.

Simon was so grateful I'd let myself go but I couldn't shake off this feeling that I shouldn't enjoy myself.

I left the hotel in the morning. I would see Simon again, years later, by which time we would both be in a very different places.

*

Although I still worked at Connie's, I started walking the Park Lane beat more frequently. Most girls weren't embarrassed and although I preferred to hide in the darkness of the night to begin with, I lost any awkward feelings pretty early you just become acclimatised, sometimes I would work in the days if it was a hot summers day, the hotter the weather, the more sexed up the men become.

I got to know the other girls and we looked for clients together, which in this area at this time, the early 80's, seemed to be extremely rich Arabian men.

Sometimes, in the summer, the sky would be lightening as the wealthy made their way home or back to hotels from exclusive nightclubs, such as Playboy. This was a good time to hang out. A client once dropped me off at dawn only for another to approach me almost straight away. He whisked me away for a champagne breakfast to the Dorchester, lovely way to end a night's work.

I preferred the backstreets around Grosvenor and Berkeley Square and sometimes, when I wanted a break, went to Gulliver's, the first black nightclub tucked in a small side street behind Park Lane.

Most of the other girls had pimps but not me. As girls returned to their beat after being paid by a client, their pimp would be waiting to take it off them. They had to earn a certain amount of money by a certain time to keep their pimp happy and they'd do bargain basement quickies to try and pile up the cash – they were under so much pressure.

As a result, sometimes one of them would tell me to get the fuck off their patch but I gave back as good as I got and pretended I had a pimp who'd already killed for me and would have no hesitation in doing so again. I got a reputation for being feisty and hardly had any trouble, something that was reinforced when I was walking nearby Gulliver's Nightclub.

I was wearing a beautiful black and white chiffon dress, which I'd bought for £200 from an old school Jewish retailer in Shepherds Bush. I adored it and was looking forward to showing it off to some friends at Gulliver's - I wasn't actually working that night.

A car pulled up beside me and two uniform policewomen got out.

One of them asked: "What are you doing?" in an aggressive tone, which immediately rubbed me up the wrong way.

"None of your fucking business," I shot back. After all, I was doing nothing wrong.

"What's your name?"

"I'm not going to tell you."

One of them grabbed my arm and I pulled away, I was taller and stronger so she lost her grip. Then they both grabbed me.

"You're under arrest for resisting arrest," one of them told me.

"What? That doesn't even make sense!"

I was furious now and kicked out as they dragged me away, catching one of them hard on the shin, causing them to cry out.

It was only then that I thought I should have just given them my name and gone on my way. Even so, I had committed no crime, simply on my way out to party. Suddenly I was in a police station being charged with assault.

In court, the officer who arrested me said: "As we were driving along Park Lane, we witnessed the defendant in a doorway stopping men and accosting them physically as they walked by."

I was appalled. This was a lie, through and through and she had sworn on the Bible she was telling the truth! Not only had I never 'accosted' a man, ever! I never picked any man up from Park Lane itself, because it was so exposed. It was totally made up and this experience instilled in me a distrust of the police (although I've since met some very nice police officers).

I ended up with a fine plus costs for medical treatment to the officer's shin: £180. It was worth every penny.

Around this time I signed up to Sophisticats escort agency, run by Jewish 'Len' a slimy guy with thinning hair and a gap in his teeth. He'd been thrown out of his posh golf club after being exposed as a pimp by the News of the world newspaper.

He made me 'audition'.

"I have to know that my girls can deliver what my clients need."

So I took my top off, grabbed his cock and gave him a hand-job he wouldn't forget in a hurry.

By this time I was 17 and had really started to find my feet in London's sexual underworld.

# Eight

# MARRIED

I used the money I got from Francesco to move to the Londonderry Hotel, where I met 'Farik' in the lobby. He was handsome, with dark, curly hair, moustache, tight-fitting open-necked shirt and an expensive, closely cut suit.

He knew what I did, took me for a drink, and he became a client. The next morning, I woke up to find Farik gone, but he'd left an envelope full of cash by the door. We went out soon after. Farik told me he was from Lebanon, but now lived between London and Paris. He introduced me to the world of casinos and taught me how to gamble; he was charming and smart and I was soon smitten. When I told him I wanted to be a singer he gave me an envelope with £700 inside and told me it was to make a demo tape.

Around a Year after we met, Farik proposed and I accepted. As I was not quite 18 yet, I needed my father's permission, so we travelled together to Bradford. Understandably, Dad had been unhappy about the way I'd left home and at first it was a little awkward between us, but soon it all settled, we still loved one another and I'd always kept in touch with dad (and my brother) since leaving home, letting him know I was okay, that I had a safe place to live, a job (although I didn't tell him what I did) and friends.

Dad, being old-fashioned, insisted that Farik and I could not sleep in the same room in his house until we were married. Dad was still dad – I couldn't even bring myself to smoke in front of him. But Farik was charming, a perfect gentleman and soon dad had to admit he was having a hard time trying to find reasons why we shouldn't be married.

Plus, Farik was incredibly wealthy – he gave me diamonds and necklaces and jewellery. I didn't even realise they were real diamonds until dad said it was dangerous to wear them around town. To prove it, he took the necklace I was wearing to a jeweller to be valued, one piece alone was worth £9,000, This was in 1980, when you could buy a small house in Bradford for less.

With dad's blessing secured, I married Farik in a registry office and moved in to his huge flat in Wetherby Place, South Kensington. In less than three years I'd gone from chamber-maid to clip joint hostess, to street walker, before marrying and moving into a swanky Kensington flat with cleaners and servants.

To my surprise, I quickly fell pregnant, three months in, I miscarried. "You're on the verge of miscarrying and it's potentially life-threatening to you. We can give you an abortion right now."

The doctor and I were on the same page, but he didn't give me much of a choice. I could have tried waiting it out, but at the same time I was so young, I wasn't ready for a child and it was clear that this was what the doctor thought.

I was in love with Farik and I was in love with the life; at 17 I didn't see marriage as something serious. On the other hand, Farik really professed to love me, which I found suffocating. I made him work hard as a result – after all I was still a teenager. I didn't want to wear long dresses and do what I was told. I wanted to wear killer heels, short skirts, low cut tops and party night and day. I was a rebel. I used to think: "How dare he tell me what to do? I'll show him!" and would find something even more daring to wear. When someone tries to box me in after I've made up my mind, it only makes it worse.

Farik was always out on business and, at a moment's notice, would leave me alone for days at a time, which suited me just fine. As a young black woman, I stood out in wealthy society and I loved it.

He once disappeared on business during the middle of a friend's party. It was in a huge Mayfair apartment, hosted by a mind-bogglingly wealthy Arab man with a diamond studded Rolex and half-dozen bodyguards.

He took me to one side and told me he was into black girls, that he wanted me and would pay handsomely to have me. He was so wealthy, I wondered whether I should in fact be with him rather than Farik. Intrigued, I gave in. True to expected form, he was very quick – straightforward. There was no foreplay, no extras, we had to be quick in case Farik came back – I found it incredibly exciting. Afterwards he handed me £5,000 in cash, still in its plastic seal, straight from the bank. Per minute, this was an extraordinarily good rate.

"If there are other girls like you Natalie," he said, "I'd be delighted to meet them."

My marriage survived this first incident, but this wealthy man and his friends still wanted me to get them black girls. I still didn't know that many hookers so brought girls I'd met at the hotel.

"Just come to the party."

"I don't know…"

"There's champagne and so on, just a great party in a huge Mayfair flat and then it's up to you."

Every now and then one of them would go off and have sex with one of the men and then they'd be given them their 'taxi fare', which came to several hundred pounds.

A bit slow off the mark, it was only a week or so later that I realised I could be making money out of this and so started taking a cut from the 'cab fares' as my introduction fee.

*

There was no way, as an ambitious 17-year-old, that I was ever going to play the role of the good wife. I was addicted to the buzz of walking Park Lane and even though I was still married and living with Farik and had everything provided for me, I decided to hit the streets again.

This involved an element of risk, as my beat was where Farik operated his business. Luckily, I was always picked up quickly, usually the moment I stepped out of a cab another car would pull up and ask for business.

A lot of girls under the control of pimps weren't very attractive and therefore spent a long time walking. Sometimes I'd chat to one of them and a guy would pull up asking for me. I'd try to get him to take both of us, even though he didn't want her, just to try and get the other girl a little money so she wouldn't get grief from her pimp.

I loved the work – I knew it was dangerous but I loved the thrill of having survived another night, then coming home and counting out my cash. It was like battling lions in the coliseum and emerging victorious every night. One night two young guys came for me and I went back with them on my own. Nothing bad happened but it was perhaps only a matter of time - this was a dangerous profession. Girls were beaten, abused and on rare occasions murdered.

Julie was picked up with another hooker, Jackie, on Park Lane.

The client was a bodybuilder, who thanks to years of overdosing on steroids had lost his mind but when he picked them up, he ticked all the right boxes. He was young, not bad looking and drove a nice car. They were in the car when the man asked Jackie to pass him something that was lying on the floor. She picked up the heavy object, which was wrapped in a blanket and handed it to the man, who was sitting in the driver's seat. He drew the blanket away to reveal a shotgun, and promptly blew Jackie's brains out. Julie managed to kick out the back windscreen, climbed out and ran, successfully, for her life. It was big news all over the Television and the News Papers. When she told me what had happened she said she didn't know where she found the strength to do this – or the speed to get away in time. Amazingly, undeterred, Julie continued to work Park Lane, propped up with prescribed medication to deal with her trauma, that would have been the last time I ever stepped back on the pavements of Park Lane, had it been me.

Even though I had access to Farik's money, I still liked making my own. I bought expensive clothes, designer handbags, watches, diamonds, necklaces - and I sent money home to my family.

After one visit back to see Dad and my brother in Bradford, it struck me that I was spending a lot of my hard earned money on expensive hotels. I found a house in Birkenshaw and bought it for £24,000. I also bought my first car.

Farik introduced me to the world of Mayfair casinos and I would end up being approached - sometimes men tossed me £100 chips while I was sitting at the blackjack or roulette table to get my attention. But they could see how much money I was spending – I wasn't going to come cheap, if I even had a price. Although the casinos let girls work there, I never worked that way. I only went to gamble. I became as addicted to gambling as I was to hooking and blew a lot of cash on the tables of the Mayfair Casinos, the more money I made the more I gambled, I was addicted.

Despite my financial recklessness, I managed to put some cash towards making demo tapes, as I still thought music was where my future lay.

Farik suspected I was still seeing other men, after all I was going out every night, but I just didn't discuss it.

Whenever Farik pulled his disappearing act, which was often, I went out to work.

# Nine

# WHAT'S GOING ON

I don't know how Cool Black, but he certainly lived up to his title, black as coal and has cool and smooth as silk, got his name but he was definitely both of those things; he was also a buck-toothed man from Grenada in his late 20's who dealt drugs to the stars. Anyone famous who needed to score was sent to see the ever trustworthy, eternally well-stocked Cool Black.

At this time 'freebasing' was in fashion. Freebasing is essentially crack but, at this time, the preparation involved made it expensive – the coke needed to be washed in ether, which was really hard to get – and dangerous. But by the end of the process, the coke was pure as could be and got you higher than a monk on a mountain.

Cool had a ritual by which he'd teach his clients how to freebase and not get killed doing it. He was utterly indispensable to the rich and famous.

We met for the first time at a party and quickly became good friends, we'd hang out together. I never saw him with a woman but I had no idea if he was gay, he certainly didn't send out that vibe.

I was at home alone in South Kensington when Cool called to say he wanted to come over and that he had a special surprise for me.

What on earth could it be? Apart from what he was most famous for, his quality Charlie.

The door buzzer rang, I opened the door in anticipation.

There was Cool B, and another guy, 'hi Cool, come in' he had another guy with him, the guy looked familiar but I just couldn't place him.

"This is Marvin," Cool said as they walked in, Next to him was a handsome man with a neatly trimmed beard.

"Hi-ya, how you doing?" the man said, kissing me on both cheeks.

It was Marvin Gaye! Did I hear Cool correctly! Of course I did! I could see it was Marvin for myself! Shit! They both sat down and I offered them a drink, reminding myself that he was just a person – and that's how he was – no pretensions, allusions.

Cool asked if he could use my kitchen to wash his charlie, a term used when you get rid of all the impurities in the coke, in order to smoke it, crack cocaine without the shit in it. I followed him.

"How- why-?"

"Marvin needs to be somewhere where no one knows him."

When I went back in Marvin was flicking through my record collection. I wanted to tell him that he was my hero, but felt foolish. His presence was enough to make me high.

He did some coke and laid his head on my lap, he seemed, it all seemed, as if we'd both known each other all our lives, without sounding too romantic. I stroked his head while he enjoyed his high.

They both didn't stay long, we talked about music, I wanted so much to say how much I'd enjoyed his music growing up, but what I didn't want to do was make him feel harassed, so I contained myself.

Eventually Marvin and Cool decided go to Tramps,

(maybe I was just a stop over to get high, didn't matter to me, I had met Marvin flipping Gaye) the most expensive nightclub in town. As he left, Marvin patted me on the bottom. "That's a fine ass you got; you work that thing girl!"

A few days later Marvin invited me to join him at Tramps. He liked my attention, it was never sexual and I never made a big deal out of his fame, we were just friends, although the lines got a bit blurred in the future.

I didn't know what to make of what had just occurred, all that I knew was that the encounter that just occurred would always be one of the a highlights of my life, it made me think of home back in Bradford, I know! I thought I voiced out loud, I'll go for a visit, hubby was hardly home, I felt hungry for something, I was easily bored, I was starting to feel like a lonely married woman, what was really happening was that subconsciously, I was about to sabotage myself.

*

When I visited Bradford to see how my family were doing, I sometimes bumped into Rudi while out clubbing, and as a young girl I'd always watched all the older girls swoon all over him, I at that tender age had already made a mental note that one day he would be mine, although I had absolutely no idea how that was going to happen. Rudi was tall, handsome, and very charming, a man I'd admired from afar back then as a child, he was still just as gorgeous as I'd remembered, even though he was some 10 years older than me.

Now I was older – and wealthier, made clear by my gold and diamond necklaces and rings, mink coat and all the other trappings that my hard earned cash had afforded me,

I was now the Yorkshire girl that had made it, I was the queen bee, but underneath my persona all I wanted was to be excepted, always afraid of being the outcast, like back in my school days, then one day by sheer coincidence ( lots of those in my life) having met up with Victor an ex-lover of my old friend Sandra, he invited me to a friends of his for a drink, and I'm guessing with an idea to getting into my rich bitch knickers, it was on an council estate, with a reputation that only the quick survived, I had no idea that it was Rudi' flat, once I arrived and realised it was his place I was although surprised I was surprisingly indifferent, he wasn't really living up to my imagination of him, there he was ironing a shirt, on a clapped out ironing board, and every now and then checking how his tin of sardines were getting along on the cooker. I sat there while Rudi, victor and another guy conversed, at some point Rudi dished out plates of sardine and rice, I was offered but declined. He wasn't quite what I'd imagined all those years ago, I had heard that he was married and inquired where his wife was. He was now divorced, good! I thought no one to get in my way if I choose to at least fuck him before I go back to London, at some point we all gathered ourselves and went out to a late night party.

As I drank the night away, I decided to make my move, 'I'm off now do you want a lift back we can share a taxi' 'cool' he replied and we left, I knew he wanted me by now and I sure desired him. I booked a hotel and the rest is history as I quickly fell head over heels in love with him. He was closer to my age, great in bed, or I at least had convinced myself of that, because in all the Years that we were together, I had never had an orgasm with him, which goes to show how MUCH! Love in a relationship conquers all the short coming. I really thought he was the one, but there was a huge problem, I was married and hubby was in

41

love with me but I now wasn't with him, Rudi would come to London and I would see him in a hotel, well that went on for a few months, but I couldn't bare not being with him and I couldn't do without him, I was addicted, besotted, I wasn't a huge smoker and was now chain smoking, full of anxiety every time I thought of him, he was my undercover lover. I couldn't bare my husband touching me anymore, only one option left give up my marriage, give up all the security, stability, everything, for Rudi, boy! He must have worked on me as I now reflect, but at that time that's what I wanted. I had booked Rudi into a B&B that was conveniently across the Rd from my home, he would sometimes come over if I knew my husband wasn't going to be back for a few days as he spent long periods away. One day my husband arrived home, I just couldn't take it anymore, he'd suspected that something was wrong in our relationship, 'it's over' I told him, it wasn't a pleasant experience especially for him, but I was adamant, he packed up a few things and left, someone would come back with his driver and pick up the rest of his belongings. I wasn't sad I was full of relief and excited with what lay ahead, I could have Rudi 24/7 now. All my security had gone, but it didn't matter, I had to crack on, it was a new adventure.

Today me and my now ex-husband are the best of friends, he remarried has beautiful children, I don't regret leaving him, in a way I may have done him a big favour.

## Ten

# END OF AN AFFAIR

Hubby moved out and although he still gave me some money, I was on my own again. If I was going to continue living in the style to which I'd become accustomed, I needed to find a way to make more money.

These were, for me, lean times, especially once the lease on Wetherby Place expired and I moved to a flat in Montague Square, (Rudi in tow) in London's West End. The flat was dark, on the ground floor with a nice garden square in front. It was a bit dismal and I had to give the estate agent a wank to get it - I had no references and he guessed what I was up to, he totally took advantage, I'm sure it was something he did regularly, little shit. I was soon making a good income from hooking but - thanks to my gambling – I struggled financially so I couldn't afford to refuse less appealing clients.

I always looked forward to seeing new clients; whenever the doorbell rang I felt a rush of excitement. Unfortunately, my hopes were often dashed.

On one occasion I threw open the door to see a sweaty, fat, moon headed, red-faced man.

"Hello," he said in an Irish accent. "My name's Patrick, we spoke on the phone."

He reeked of alcohol.

My face fell. 'Oh God,' I thought, 'Give me strength.'

When I needed the money, there were clients I saw in whom I just could not find any redeeming feature. Patrick was one of them.

Up until this point I hadn't done anything in the way of proper domination, but I enjoyed 'mistreating men' when they asked for it. Patrick liked to be spanked on the bottom with a wooden paddle.

He started to undress.

"Shall we start with a massage?" he said.

He had a fat back covered in white spots that popped as I rubbed. It seemed as though he never washed. As I massaged in the oil, an overpowering smell of stale urine wafted up. While Patrick, lying face down, moaned in pleasure, I silently mouthed the words: 'You stinking, disgusting fat fuck, you don't pay me nearly enough for this.'

As soon as I could afford not to see him, Patrick would be the first to go.

I didn't know what he did at first – I assumed he was a prison warden because he had an enormous bunch of keys that he always placed on the bedside table and always asked me to remind him to collect them when he left.

One day, he was undressing when something fell from his neck.

"Oh God!" he exclaimed and he snatched something up off the floor and wrapped it on his clothes. It was a priest's collar. I pretended not to see it but I was amazed. A priest, wow. Nothing would shock me after this. It summed up the power of men's needs in an instant – if a priest couldn't control his urges what man could?

With every strike of the paddle Patrick would cry out: "Oh God, please forgive me! God loves me! Tell me what a naughty boy I've been! Oh God! Punish the naughty boy! Jesus Christ save me! Oh God, Oh God, Oh God!"

I've always believed in God and still do. I think he's been there, protecting me in my leanest and most difficult times – but he tested me with Patrick.

Patrick wasn't the only religious man I saw. I once opened the door to find an orthodox Jew in full regalia in front of me.

I tried to hide my surprise and welcomed him inside. He wanted a massage, so he undressed and peeled off several layers of what must have been some religious-related beige cotton undergarments. He also had an unpleasant smell, like he hadn't washed for a while; he barely said a word during the whole session.

I'm a trooper – I was always going to make whatever money I needed to survive. When a man's standing in front of you, turning them away feels like throwing away a thick wad of much-needed cash - but I would never do anything I really couldn't face. For example, I never had unprotected sex with a client.

I still strolled to the backstreets of Park Lane. One night I noticed that a car had been circling around the same streets. A nervous client, I thought at first, but the car stopped and the driver spoke to a girl in a Curzon Street doorway before driving off again.

He appeared a few minutes later and I heard a girl shout "Time waster," before she slammed his car door and drove off. That didn't happen very often. I assumed he was most likely a cheapskate.

I was more experienced by this time and had learned how things usually went down – from playing cat and mouse with the police (I'd usually make sure to stand where I could spot them coming from a long way off) to spotting time wasting clients.

A few minutes later I saw the same car again, and this time he stopped to talk to me. I wasn't having any of it.

"Why don't you just fuck off?"

"No, no, please, can I talk to you?"

"It'll cost you £80."

"Alright."

"Now."

"Okay."

This was a steep price back then but he agreed without hesitation and handed over the cash, so I got in and slammed the door. He said his name was Christopher; he was dressed in jacket and corduroy trousers and was a scrawny, thin-faced pale man. I'd later found out he was in his mid-30s but he looked much older, like a cross between Michael Palin and Bill Nighy.

He drove to his flat in Manson's Place, a quiet mews off Queensgate in South Kensington. It was total squalor inside. I asked to use the bathroom, which was next to the kitchen and both were practically no-go areas – every glass, every piece of crockery was lined with mould and there was a black-rimmed tub and grimy tiled floor in the bathroom.

Christopher told me he was an art dealer and owned a shop on Brompton Street. It was extraordinary. I just couldn't match the man in front of me to the squalor of this apartment. I found his record collection and was at least pleased to see it included some Marvin Gaye.

The bedroom was practically empty; dark very dingy, there was just a mattress on the floor. We got undressed. He was so scrawny – he had the body of an old man.

The sex turned out to be anything but ordinary.

"I want you to squash my head between your thighs."

"Okay." I was used to the old unusual request and was game.

"Harder, harder, harder!"

Okay, I thought, he's a fucking weirdo but if that's what he wants for his £80, then fine by me.

Then he told me to say certain phrases and insults - things, like: "You're a dirty white shit!" I soon caught on and started shouting abuse at him. He told me to smack him across the face and then spit in his mouth. Then I pulled his hair while I spanked his arse with paddles and he inhaled amyl nitrate, and I then followed that by caning him until he bled. I was amazed at how much pain Chris was able to take and wondered if he perhaps some kind of problem with his nerves.

Chris became a regular after that and although I saw him at least once a week I found out very little about his private life, initially, I could never telephone him - he had to call me, until he started to trust me, then I could call him.

The only thing I knew about him was that he had a sister who had a psychological disorder and that he had another home in Barnes after he went there one night to get some cash to pay me. I could never call him and when he was out of slave mode, he wasn't pleasant at all, as if he didn't even like me that much.

That first night, I left Christopher's place on a strange high – buzzing from having survived another extraordinary and extreme experience. I'd emerged victorious from the lion's den once more.

I should perhaps have known then that there was trouble ahead but at that time, as far as I was concerned, Christopher paid well, so who was I to complain?

*

Out of all the well-known faces I would get to know in an unusual manner, Marvin Gaye was top of my list, my childhood hero.

So it was a pleasant surprise having not seen Marvin for a very long time, that he was now living in the very same apartment block as me, Park West apartments.

I had moved from the dingy flat in Montague Sq. and moved to Park West. I had heard from the doorman that Marvin had moved in, he gave me the flat number and at some point I'd pay him a visit, but I didn't need to, a few days later I bumped into him as he was coming into the building and I was leaving, 'Hi Marvin do you remember me? "Sure I do Natalie, how ya doin?" "Great!" I replied, 'we live in the same block' 'really Nat, cool, come over and party tonight' he said with a glint in his eyes, Rudi was in Bradford, I had mentioned that I'd met Marvin in the past and he was rather impressed, he did enquire if I and Marvin had been intimate and at that time my answer was no, as that had been the case then. Later on that evening I put on a silk blue dress and went round to his apartment, Marvin let me in, another girl was there when I arrived. She was Dutch, beautiful, blonde and slim. She was dressed in stockings, suspenders and high heels and nothing else. They'd been freebasing cocaine. I sat feeling quite awkward, this wasn't a booking, I watched as she pulled on the glass pipe and after exhaling she beckoned me over with her finger.

"You like girls, don't you Natalie?" Marvin asked. "Go to her. She's my bitch. Do whatever you want." and so I went over to her, the room smelt of cocaine, it must be travelling out into the communal corridors, I was slightly concerned, but they weren't so why should I be, so I walked over to her.

She pulled again on the pipe and I locked my lips on hers. She blew into my mouth and we started to kiss passionately, wrapped in smoke. She, and I caressed high on coke, then she being directed, by the director sitting in the corner telling her what to do, started to undress me, I was excited but felt a little awkward with Marvin watching.

Then at some point, Marvin came over, and started spanking her lightly on her bottom, she was by now on her knees, going down on me. He called her a bitch, a dirty bitch, he didn't say it in a menacing way, more in a seductive sexual tone, he came over and then slid into her from behind. This had all happened in a rather swift fashion, the coke hadn't given me much time to process much of this 'ménage à trois' situation I'd now found myself in, from the moment I took a pull on the pipe I was now a part in Marvin' fantasies. He called me over to him and we gently kissed.

When he'd had enough of her, he said: "Use her. But don't abuse her." In his soft sexy mellow American accent, eventually he went back to his chair, lit his pipe and sat watching the two of us 'get it on' Marvin always had a slightly glazed look in his eyes, as though, present in body but his mind elsewhere, constant look of inquisitiveness.

She did whatever Marvin wanted with zeal.

And I didn't leave for two days, thank goodness I didn't have far to travel when I did…..

The last time I saw Marvin was at a party at a famous soul singer's West End flat. The coke ran out at 6am. I volunteered to get some more and the soul singer gave me the address of a dealer. Marvin decided to come with me.

Dawn was just breaking as we hailed a cab to go to an address, which turned out to be a large and dangerous-looking estate. I gave the cabbie a good tip and asked him to wait.

"No problem."

"Do you know who that is?" I asked as Marvin walked ahead. "Do you recognise him? That's Marvin Gaye." I said showing off.

"Yeah, yeah, I recognise him. Look, how long are you going to be?"

"Fifteen minutes."

I caught up with Marv, as he was eager to get to where he was heading pronto! As we walked an idea hit me, well, it was more than an idea it had been a lifelong fantasy, never for a millisecond any real belief it could ever be a possibility

"Marvin?"

"Yeah."

'Ok… I know this is going to sound silly' I had to ask, it was now or never, when would I ever get this opportunity again

'Could we sing a duet, right now?'

"Sure. What do you want to sing?"

"You Are Everything?"

I cleared my throat and started to sing and he sang back, 'today I saw some somebody'…….. It had been a long night and our throats weren't at their freshest but, as he held my hand and we sang in the summer dawn, on our way to score some cocaine, I had taken Diana Ross' part and it was the Nat and Marvin show, I thought this had to be one of the most serene moments of my life, and it WAS an unforgettable moment that I'll cherish forever.

Marvin died young, shot dead by his own father during an argument at his family home the day before his 45th birthday in 1984. I cried when Rudi told me the news; it was a huge shock to all that knew and loved him, I was so fond of Marvin, his music lives on, and at least I had the privilege of singing with a soul legend.

*

June, a hooker friend of mine, introduced me to Madam C, a onetime hooker who'd become one of London's top Madams. The 'C' stood for Caroline; she was an alcoholic Irish lady who was always sloshed to the extent that she'd often forget to collect her fees from her girls. She lived in a flat in Maida Vale in West London and had an Iranian boyfriend.

When I first started working for her she was in control of her business but she gradually started to slip over time, as the booze got the better of her.

I was only one of three non-white girls on her books and Madam C sent me to a client whether they asked for a black girl or not. My colour was never an issue; I was never rejected because I was black. I was young, good-looking and the clients were always delighted when they saw me on their doorstep.

Madam C didn't advertise. Her clients got to her by word of mouth and she catered for a huge range of people from the upper echelons of society – the arts, politics, as well as the landed gentry.

As well as Madam C, I was still working Park Lane and the hostess club but Madam C paid best. The average price was £1,500 and Caroline took a third. She also took me under her wing, in that she taught me everything she knew about pleasing men outside of the bedroom.

Take my clothes coordination for example. I tended to go for bright colours, short dresses and plunging necklines. She advised me to go to certain shops: "Let the assistants assist, darling, that's what they're there for."

And then cuisine: "When you eat in a restaurant with a client, eat like they do, with your knife finger like so, along the knife and you should hold your fork as close to the end of the handle as possible. The closer to the end, the more successful you will be in life."

"Don't ask clients for money. Money matters are vulgar and ugly. But of course we want to bleed the gentleman dry of cash, so flatter them. They know it's a game but the way you do it makes all the difference."

She taught me how to select wine, to match certain types with certain foods, and how to hold a wine glass. "It's not a pint glass darling, cradle it in one hand, thus," she'd say, swirling her glass which was full of whisky, "and sip it silently, let it wet your lips so they glisten in the candlelight."

She once reprimanded me for saying 'posh'. "Never use that word darling, never. 'Posh' people do not use it to describe themselves, only common people do – and you, darling, are anything but common."

She was as fiery as she was disoriented and ran the agency with ruthless chaos. She'd be counting out thousands of pounds in the lounge and would get up to refresh her drink in the kitchen and forget about the money, leaving it lying there in front of me or some other girl.

Sometimes she'd be distracted by a row with her Iranian boyfriend, rows in which she would quickly turn violent and ended with Madam C throwing bottles at the poor man's head. I liked Caroline but I could see she was in the twilight years of her profession. She'd been going for so long she had the complete and utter trust of her clients, and was constantly busy, despite the hiccups.

She never meant to give her girls her clients' numbers but she started getting careless and gave them to me, so I'd tell them to call me directly, meaning I got all the cash. If I were busy elsewhere, I'd set them up with another girl.

Madam C sent me to see an older gentleman and he became a regular of mine. He had so much money it defied belief. Each time I was sent to a different address, fabulous mansions in Chelsea, Knightsbridge and Belgravia, all owned by him, all with bodyguards outside. The first time I saw him I made £2,000.

"You seem like a switched on girl," he told me one day.

"Madam C's been a bit erratic these past few months. Can you get me girls?"

Fellow hooker Michelle, who also wanted to be singer, suggested I ask him for £20,000 so I could cut a demo album.

"Don't be ridiculous!"

"It's nothing to him and he loves you. If you don't ask, you don't get."

So I asked. He looked at me for a moment, went into another room and came back with £20,000 in a carrier bag. It was like 20p to him. You could buy a flat in Mayfair for £40,000 at this time but, unfortunately, I blew it all in the Victoria Grosvenor casino.

Gambling was my one weakness. With that much 'free' cash I wasn't able to help myself and went whenever I had free time between bookings, playing blackjack and roulette until it was all gone. It was a compulsion. It cleared my mind. I didn't need the money – I wasn't gambling to win. Gambling was a means of escape for me.

I needed to escape from Rudi. He had moved in with me and once he knew the kind of money I was making, he said he was happy to be a kept man. When he complained I was driving a better car than he was – a Burgundy Jaguar – I gave it to him after Christopher bought me a gold BMW.

I also gave Rudi tens of thousands of pounds even though he was violent towards me. There were good times as well - and I was blinded by love - so didn't leave him. Despite the risks, I wanted Rudy's baby, but suffered a bad miscarriage that nearly cost me my life.

Apart from gambling, another means of escape came via some clients. One notable man was Phillip, whom I met through Madam C. He gave me his real name from the start. He was tall, 7 years older than me, he had a pageboy haircut, and he'd booked me to be his 'girlfriend' at a party, he paid me up front, the booking consisted of me accompanying him to a party, ok, I thought this is different, I'll go along with it, he was extremely charming with a gentle disposition about him.

Phillip didn't seem to mind that I was black, and stuck out like a sore thumb at this party, although I felt very self-conscious when we arrived at this very posh all-white party in a terraced house in Chelsea, I kept my composer. The door was open and people had spilled out into the front garden onto the pavement.

I was met with curious stares and did my best to play the role, telling people I was a singer. Did some of his pals know that I was being paid? Was it some sort of bet? Maybe not, maybe he just wanted a date to bring along, I was treated well by his friends and soon forgot I was even on a booking, Phillip put me at ease and I partied and drank the night away. When Phillip learned that singing was my real passion, he was quite surprised that I wasn't just a hooker and that I had other ambitions and wanted to do something else.

I'm certain that when he first called up, he thought it would just be a one-off – he wasn't even sure he would sleep with me - but he did. Then he booked me again for a restaurant date, and our relationship developed. He was young, not bad looking, had been to Harrow and was clearly going to be someone important.

I liked him and he kept booking me for other 'dates'. It was a bit awkward. If we'd met independently of the job (which would have been highly unlikely) we could have had a normal boyfriend/girlfriend relationship but because of who I was and who he was, he had to pay me if he wanted to see me again. I've always had a niggling thought, when I look back on our encounter, that I may have been Phillips first ever sexual encounter, had he been a virgin?

Hmm guess I'll never know, if so I hope it put him in good stead.

After our dates, Phillip would usually end up taking me back to his home in Chelsea ; there was an older woman there, probably his mother, we were never introduced, She didn't like me at all (they never do). I arrived and Phillip and I quickly disappeared upstairs.

The house was packed full of old furniture, - back then I just thought 'why don't they just buy some new stuff?' – It all looked like old second-hand tat to me. Obviously, I know now that they were all incredibly valuable antiques. Phillip' bedroom was cozy, however. I loved being there; his bedside lamp gave out a mellow light.

One day he booked me to come around and told me: "I'm so sorry but I can't see you anymore, I have to end it."

I was upset, he wasn't obliged at all to tell me in person, it was kind of him, our arrangement had become blurred or at least that's what I thought had but an end to it. I liked him, enjoyed chilling in his room, talking and eating out. But he did it nicely. He said he'd become addicted to me and it wasn't healthy. I suspected that his mother had made him do it.

A few years later I was tidying up my flat with the TV on in the background when I heard Phillips name, Phillip Oppenheim. This was at the time when the BBC had just started showing parliamentary proceedings live on TV. I stopped what I was doing and couldn't believe it when I saw Phillip stand up to speak. He had lost some of his hair but there was no mistaking him. I was delighted to see he was doing so well. I smiled and wondered to my self was that the real reason he had ended our 'relationship' was it because he was going into Politics? Or was he at the time already a Politician?

Just as amazingly, the debate happened to be about

something that I was interested in. "Don't be a hypocrite now," I thought as he started to speak, but he seemed to be on the right side as far as I was concerned.

I was tempted to get in touch, but thought this might shock him – or think I was up to something sinister. I later heard from another client down the Years that Phillip had opened a restaurant in Fulham and was tempted to pop in but I reconsidered, I didn't want to put him in an awkward position. I'm not saying things would have necessarily been different otherwise, but our respective careers have definitely kept us apart. Phillip served in various ministerial posts in the Thatcher and Major Governments, as well as aide to a senior Cabinet Minister. Politician or not he was a gent and kind to me.

Another wonderful client from this time was a woman, who introduced me to cocaine,

Drugs – especially cocaine - were all around me at this time but I'd not touched any since I was fifteen and working Park Lane. I met a famous musician from an R&B-funk-disco group, The Crown Heights Affair at Gulliver's nightclub and we went back to his room at the Drury Lane Hotel.

"Have a line."

"No, I don't do that."

"Go on, just a small one. Just taste it to start with."

I put a little bit on my finger and dabbed it on my tongue. I thought it tasted disgusting and didn't want to do it, even after my tongue went a bit numb.

He carried on insisting and eventually wore me down. I sniffed a small line and my throat went numb and I couldn't swallow. I just didn't get it. I couldn't understand why he wanted to put some on my tits and suck it off.

Being in this line of work it was all around me – everyone I knew was into freebasing, an expensive and dangerous habit and I steered clear of cocaine until the day I received a request from Madam C to visit a bisexual woman who lived in Park Crescent, at the top of Regent's Park. Great address, I thought, but the booking was for the following morning at 7am, and I wasn't a morning person. I arrived sleepy-eyed and a uniformed housekeeper let me in. It was like ascending a stairway to heaven – everything in white, gold and so much space (there was a concert grand piano in the lounge); it was all so clean, so perfect.

I was led into a beautiful white bedroom and sat there beautiful, tanned and blonde was Christine.

"Hello, you must be Natalie," she said as I stifled a yawn.

She spoke in a soft Scottish accent. She was tanned, had a slight gap in her front two teeth; was quite short with wavy blonde hair and was about ten years older than me. She wore a watch studded with diamonds on a gold bangle a gold ring with a huge diamond, an emerald necklace and nothing else

"Sorry, I'm not early riser," I answered.

"Don't worry, we'll soon wake you up." She leaned across the enormous circular bed, opened a bedside drawer and took out a large clear plastic bag of white powder. There must have been three or four ounces inside.

"And would you like any breakfast?"

A maid brought in softly scrambled eggs and chipolatas. It was delicious – I'd only ever had scrambled eggs that had been cooked until they were rock solid, these were soft and creamy.

"Let's eat first and then party," Christine said. "And by the way here's your envelope." I didn't count it. Madam C had taught me that was inappropriate. I just put it in my bag and could feel the bulge was substantial enough.

Then came the coke. Christine cut me a line and I

managed to snort it while Christine fetched some champagne and, once I got over the numbness, I started to feel pretty good – now I got it.

I got down to my bra and knickers and got into bed with Christine. Life! One minute I'd been curled up in bed at home, all sleepy and now I was in bed with blonde dripping in jewels while I was coked off my nuts.

Christine was a high-class hooker who was being kept by a very rich man, for his exclusive use. He owned properties all over central London but he'd given this one to Christine.

She patted the bed. "Get in."

So I did. And we started to make love. It was fantastic, the coke made everything from the sheets to Christine's skin feel impossibly wonderful – and my energy went through the roof. The bed rotated as we kissed and rolled around together and when I looked up at the ceiling, I could see Christine's initials had been worked into the plaster.

Christine paid £400, part of which went to Madam C, but Christine booked me separately after that, for £250 a time. She was always very respectful towards me. She even let me drive her Rolls Royce. I loved the attention that I got - people were looking at me and wondering how on earth a young black girl like myself could be driving such a car. I wanted to be rich enough to afford my own Rolls.

She also took me to Annabel's nightclub. This was an extremely highbrow club, it wasn't enough to be fabulously wealthy – to be a member here you had to be somebody of great importance. Annabel's was the sort of place where Royals could go and be left alone.

I saw Christine often at home in Eton Square, Portland Place and Holland Park and met all of her friends, most of who seemed to be post-1979-revolutionary exiles from

Iran. All of them were into freebasing coke. We grew quite close for a time and Christine let me bring my friends around to show off.

It was around this time that I decided – as I was going from strength to strength - that it was time to start my own agency. I was now 21-years-old.

I had a long standing friendship with Christine down the Years, she no longer paid me we, had become friends, the last time I saw Christine, she had fallen on hard times, I'd noticed her life unravelling once her sugar daddy had left the scene, she had become more dependent on cocaine and her habit had escalated to crack cocaine. The once pristine home was now in a sorry state, gone was the maid, all her cars, homes, and pretty much all her assets, no more jewellery, and her looks had dramatically faded far too soon for her age. Christine represented my worst fear. She had had everything and through drug addiction, had lost it all, she had been some bad choices a by-product from her mind being clouded by smoke, literally. Last time I went in search for her, her last remaining property had been repossessed, and she was gone. Maybe one day I'll find her again.

## Eleven

# FREE!

I wanted to advertise in What's On and Where to Go but demand was so great the listings editor had to be bribed. It cost me £300 to get my ad (which cost £80 per week) to jump to the top of the queue. At first I thought I was going to do all the work. It quickly became too much and I had two phone lines – one for work and one for my personal life. An agency had a service where by you could divert your calls to them, they would deal with the bookings for you and they took a percentage, while I was busy and I dealt with them when I got back, when I was called directly I of course took the best bookings, for instance if the guy was staying in a 5 star hotel and he had a suite instead of a room, I couldn't get my high heels on fast enough, but it I also had to fit his or her requirements, otherwise I passed the booking onto my girls.

It was precarious for a while but, as word spread, the client list grew and grew, so much so that I became picky. If the caller didn't sound well educated or wealthy, then I wouldn't go. If I didn't like the look of where they lived or the client's appearance, I'd turn around and leave. I also got requests for certain body shapes – I could cover most things, one popular girl was girl was five feet tall with 40DD bust. Odder requests included pregnant or lactating girls.

Part of my success came from befriending and trusting my girls – I loaned them money if they were short and they worked hard for me in return. Another part of my success was that I treated my clients well and was genuinely honest and caring (which made me come across less mercenary – a lot of men said they thought they were being ripped off by other agencies) - until we reached the bedroom. Men needed to hear the right things – and sometimes very different things, but I was quick to learn what each man wanted.

Black Beauties was the first ever agency specialising in Caribbean, African and Brazilian ladies- all woman of colour, Girls called up in droves to sign up. They included Sonya, who worked for Reuters; Peggy, a Zambian coke fiend. She was in the UK illegally and couldn't read or write in English. Carol, who was from Guyana, was as cold as ice and I sent her to the cruellest, most demanding clients. Then there was Claire, very good at domination – she wasn't afraid of causing pain. Yvonne, a bisexual, was 50% black, but light-skinned with green-blue eyes. Christine was the daughter of a Nigerian diplomat and knockout beautiful until she became a crack and coke addict, at which stage I wasn't able to rely on her. If a client had coke then she'd disappear for 36hours when she was only booked for two. Sherry was a hairdresser from Trinidad and brilliant with temperamental clients. Katrina was from Brixton - one client gave her £100,000. She opened a bar but got ripped off and lost it all. I had nurses, teachers, bankers and law students who catered for my clients' every need. They were all grateful that at last they didn't feel second best – before Black Beauties they were only sent out if a client had asked for a black girl or if all the white girls were busy. We all knew black was beautiful and the success of the agency proved it at last.

I charged a minimum of £350 per session and took a commission, the higher the amount the client was paying would dictate what commission I took, I was taking in on average £15,000 a month a lot of money back then and I was small fry compared to some more established agencies and if special bookings came in much more,

Although I was now a successful madam, I still had a lot to learn about the business. There was one month, a very good month where I just couldn't get around to banking and finally walked into the building society with £40,000 in Swiss Francs, dollars and pounds. The manager took forever checking all the notes. The £50 note had just come out and the Bank of England was worried that some enterprising criminal would manage to produce a convincing forgery. He was also clearly suspicious, young girl, so much cash, and unknown to me at the time he informed the police.

I'd fallen pregnant to Rudi and was a couple of months along. Despite my previous problems, I really hoped to have Rudi's baby but I was now having a miscarriage and was rushed to hospital – the doctors said it wasn't looking good but to go home as all hope wasn't lost yet, I'd just returned home – early morning, the next day the police came crashing through my front door. I had a friend staying with me at the time and she opened the door to the cops. I had a bag of cocaine I was holding for someone, as well as quite a bit of hashish. Naively, I told the police exactly that, and this was enough for the officers to charge me with possession of a Class-A substance with intent to supply. The officers were polite and friendly, and I chatted to them about my work and my clients and, although they were genuinely interested, I should have kept quiet.

If only I'd been a bit smarter here – but I wasn't thinking straight. When the police handed me their initial statement regarding the arrest, it said that when I opened the door I was wearing a white bikini.

"That's fucking impossible!" I yelled back at them, "I'm in the middle of a threatened miscarriage; that's last thing I'd wear!"

This was stupid because they changed the story, so it was correct by the time we got to court. My body couldn't deal with the stress and I lost the baby, a blessing otherwise I'd be forever connected to Rudi, phew! Having said that, the police really weren't that bright. Although they took all my bank statements, they didn't touch my account. So I went to the bank and cleaned it out. I opened a new account in Rudi's and my names, so he could carry on paying the mortgage in Bradford if I went to jail.

I remained on bail for almost a year, so returned to Bradford to live quietly for a bit. Life with Rudi was not good. Dotted amongst the good times were many memories of savage beatings. Rudi had whipped me with a belt buckle, catching me right between the eyes after I'd had a threesome with a touring Harlem Globetrotter and another girl, for pure fun. I'd made a mistake of putting the encounter in my diary: "a wonderful weekend and didn't miss Rudi at all." As I tried to run away I caught my hand on the latch to the bathroom door, tearing off a strip of skin and then Rudi punched me as I lay on the bathroom floor while one of his friends, Teddy, said: "She deserves it!" The doctor at the hospital asked me if there was anything I wanted to tell him but I just looked ahead, staying silent as he stitched me up.

Rudi also once threw a hot cup of coffee in my face, and another occasion he left me with bruises on my back after another belt-buckle beating. He held a knife to my face when I refused to withdraw £5,000 from my bank account and hand it over to him and cut the palm of my hand to make me see he was serious. So I went, but while he was waiting outside in the car I told the cashier what had happened and they called the police. They arrested Rudi but, like many women in my position, I dropped the charges.

Then, while I was on bail, I went to a Bradford nightclub with him. We were having an okay time, we were on the stage with DJ, dancing and started to argue. He said: "I don't want any trouble from you tonight," and slapped me across the face.

He'd just slapped me in front of hundreds of people. A red mist descended. I punched Rudi as hard as I could and he fell back into the DJ booth, knocking over his decks and bringing the music to a sudden and violent stop. The house lights came on and the crowd watched as I laid into Rudi. Someone shouted: "She's lost her mind!" Rudi tried to fight back but I was all over him, fists pounding, I'd never been so angry in all my life, it took six men to pull me off him and still I wouldn't stop. I wanted blood! Rudi was, like all bullies, a coward at heart and just shied away from me after that.

This was, for me, a new beginning. I realised Rudi wasn't as strong as I thought he was. I was stronger. I didn't dump him – I should have, I know – but our relationship had changed. He knew I would fight back now, that I was as strong as he was so he needed to back off – which he did. I also knew that I was going to need a friend if I was sent to prison, someone who understood my world, and Rudi was the only person in this position.

I was eventually convicted of possession with intent to supply and sentenced to 18 months, nine suspended – which meant I would serve a minimum of six months with good behaviour. I was taken to what was then the new Cookham Wood Prison in Kent.

During my induction the officer asked me if I'd been in prison before.

"No, it's my first time."

"You're very calm about the whole thing."

"What do you want me to do? Go Crazy? Shout and scream?"

I was terrified of prison but I was not going to panic. Once I was 'checked in' I braced myself for the horror of prison life.

Then, as I entered prison on that first day, I spotted a familiar face.

Miss B!

The law's long arm had finally stretched far enough to grab even her – although I was of course delighted, because not only did it mean I had a friend but a protector, too. I could have cried with relief. She was amazing, she had girls manicuring nails and massaging her feet, I don't know how she managed but nobody ever messed with her and there were some really rough fuckers in there.

It was still hard enough being in prison, even with Miss B to take care of me. I hated being with these desperate, hard women. I had had a wonderful life out in the 'real world'. Prison was full of murderers, robbers and drug dealers and I was forced to mix with them, to try and befriend them. Those who chose to remain outsiders weren't trusted and gangs would terrorise them. Sometimes, in return for the unlucky inmate's 'protection' they'd force family members to work as drug mules. One inmate, under pressure from the gangs, persuaded her grandmother to bring in drugs and just a few months later, the grandmother was in prison too,

I hated the fact I wasn't able to get a proper mirror; they only allowed prisoners to use these plastic things, so couldn't make sure I looked okay when Dad came to visit. I asked him not to come again; it was awful for him to see me in there.

Rudi took care of the mortgage, wrote and came to see me often; we were even granted a closed visit where we could be in a room together without a guard present.

Rudi brought some hashish with him. I inserted it somewhere. The officers didn't search me when I went back to my cell and I used it as currency – it was extremely valuable inside and it went a long way to making things a little more comfortable. You could get anything you wanted in prison, including heroin and cocaine but I wasn't tempted.

The food was appalling and I was always hungry. I was always conscious of not having enough and I developed a bit of an eating disorder in that even long after I was released I'd wake up in middle of night and go and grab something to eat, that I'd stored by my bed side table.

I was presented with bucket and mop and told my job was to clean. A few days later another prisoner came up to me. I could tell she considered herself a bit of a hard case.

"Hand over your cigarettes," she demanded.

"What?"

"I'm taking your cigarettes."

I can't stand bullies, so my reaction - to hit her in the face with my wet mop - was instinctive. She got two days in isolation and I got two days of 'loss of association', which meant I could only come out of me cell to eat. After that I decided not to take any more risks, I wanted to get out with time for good behaviour.

I was reading a fashion magazine in the communal area when someone, reading over my shoulder, said: "Who's Laura Ashley?"

There was a full-page advert for the designer and I

thought to myself "Who on earth doesn't know who Laura Ashley is?"

I turned around to see an old lady standing there. She smiled at me.

"Don't talk to her," a fellow inmate said. "She's always trying to ingratiate herself with the new prisoners."

"Why shouldn't I talk to her?"

"Because she's Myra Hindley, that's why." I felt contaminated that I'd even shared the same air as that evil being.

When I mentioned this to Madam V, she sucked her teeth: "That dirty girl don' wan' cross my path."

I got the impression that Madam V would have taken great pleasure in killing Hindley – and she wasn't alone. The danger was considered so great that she almost never left her cell without an escort, and if she did, it was because the wardens let her stretch her legs late at night, when everyone else was locked in. She also had a TV in her cell, which was more than she deserved.

The rest of my time inside passed quietly and six months later, I was a free woman. To step outside into the fresh air and into Rudi's arms was a delight. The very next thing I did was go to the nearest perfume store and buy a large bottle of Coco Chanel with the last of the cash I'd had on me when I came in. The smell was like heaven in a bottle.

Next stop was the bank. Rudi waited outside.

"I'm sorry, there's nothing in your account," the cashier told me.

"Check again."

She did. There was nothing. It turned out that spending that £60 had been a bit rash as Rudi, the bastard, had cleaned me out while I was inside.

I stormed back to the car.

"Where's my fucking money?"

"We'll talk about it when we get home."

I tried to get it out of him but he wouldn't say anything, so before we got home I bought a miniature bottle of brandy to calm my nerves, hoping he'd invested it and I'd be able to sell whatever it was he'd bought.

Once we were inside he said: "I was trying to use the money to make more money for you."

"How?"

He said that he'd gambled it all away. He'd even sold the Jag. Weirdly, I kind of believed him at the time and let him get away with way too much. I'd spent so much time in love with Rudi and trying to make him love me that I'd developed a huge psychological wall I had yet to get over, which meant I was still in thrall to him. Even though I was a tough character, I crumbled before Rudi. I just didn't want to see him for the deceitful, conniving little bastard he was.

The more I thought about what he'd done, the more that wall was reduced. I'd already started to fall out of love with him after the nightclub punch-up and was able to see that the only reason he came to visit me in prison was to keep me sweet while he gambled my money away.

Then I discovered - via a friend – that Rudi hadn't gambled the money away. It was far worse: he had a whole other life that he kept secret from me. He'd used my money to buy a house for Jackie, the woman he loved and lived with in Bradford. I'd wanted to try and have children with Rudi, but this other woman had already had three kids with him – and I had worked to support them all!

I felt so used. I'd given Rudi everything but he'd used me, pimped me to get what he wanted. He had never been in love with me. If anything fuelled my ability to dominate men, it was my experience with Rudi.

That was the end of Rudi, at long last. Although I was able to grow up and move on, I know of many girls who stayed in these kind of abusive relationships; I'm just grateful that somehow I not only realised that I needed to do myself justice and leave Rudi but also found the strength to kick Rudi to one side for once and for all.

When I told Rudi it was over, he snorted in reply. He clearly didn't believe me but I didn't care. I walked away and never looked back.

I had to start from scratch. I was in my early 20s and growing up fast. Luckily, I still had some very valuable gifts that had been given to me as presents mostly jewellery, so I sold that in Hatton Garden. It was worth more than £100,000 but I let it go for less than £10,000. I suspect the jeweller couldn't believe his luck after I quickly gave in and agreed his price.

Then I caught a train to Bradford and, my only relief, was that Rudi had paid just enough of the mortgage to keep the bank from repossessing it (the house wasn't in his name), so put it straight on the market. It had nearly doubled in value. I'd bought my first home, a detached property at the age of 19, not bad for a runaway, now it was gone. While I waited for the sale to go through the bank gave me a bridging loan.

Finally, I had enough to go back into business. I was a little bit older tougher and a lot wiser – and this time nothing was going to get in my way.

# Twelve

# LIBERATED

I returned to London, found a flat in Beaumont Street in Marylebone and placed my ad in What's On And Where To Go. The woman in the flat above me was doing same thing and we paid high rent for fairly shoddy flats – the landlords knew what was going on.

It was difficult, but I kept my prices low and demand for my services grew. Since I'd left Rudi, he'd turned more violent, once showing up with a knife. He dragged me to the bank to give him some more money.

I soon moved to a much better location – a converted garage in Abbey Road, St John's Wood. Yeah! I know, but it was a fantastic conversion and an upgrade from before. The landlord was a handsome BA pilot - we slept together, not for any reason other than we fancied each other, he owned the entire building and kept one of the flats for himself. The rent was high and although I suspected he knew what I did, he never said anything and was just happy he was paid on time.

I was just heading for a night out on the town and was still on the garden path when I felt as though something was wrong. It was as if I was that little girl walking home on my own back from the pub again. I turned to go back to the house when someone grabbed me from behind and pulled me onto the grass, behind the trees and bushes. As I fought back I saw it was Rudi and, frozen by my shock for a moment, he quickly overpowered me pinned me down on my back before he pushed his face on to mine, a horrible, sickening forced kiss as he lifted my skirt; I started to cry, asking him why? Then, finally: "Why are you doing this to me? I hate you, I hate you!"

He stopped. The truth of what I said had hit him like a slap in the face. He stared into my eyes and stared back right into his soul, There was nothing he could do to get me back now. It was over and unless he was going to lock me in a dungeon there was nothing he could do to possess me anymore. He got up and ran away down the path. I had beaten my addiction to Rudi, I felt liberated, free, strong, HAPPY!

After this I moved not far from Abbey Rd., to a block of private flats in Maida Vale called the Carlton Apartments. I would move so many times, before eventually buying my own place. My favourite haunt at this time was Fidenzies nightclub in Mayfair, which had one of the late night licenses in London. A lot of hookers went there as well as lots of other 'late workers', people working the nightshift or very early shifts in local markets, hotels and hospitals, which is how the club got their license. It stayed open and served alcohol until 6am, which in those days was quite unusual and attracted celebs such as George Michael, Mickey Rourke, Chaka Khan, Soap stars and other A list celebs. I wasn't shy in approaching any of the Celebs that came to the club if I chose to, but for some reason, the one celeb I felt fazed to go up to and say hello was Jools Holland I wished I'd struck up a conversation him, he may have told me to bugger off, as my desire was to be a singer, and I was such an admirer of his musical talent, I should have risked it.

TV comedian Roland Rivron, once came back from

Fidenzies with a group of us to a party in South Kensington BOY! Could he hoover up the charlie, and not once did he put his hand to contribute to the copious amount on offer, plus he polished off the alcohol like no tomorrow. He actually had a fling with 'Blow-Job' Bella that night (Bella once made a bet that she could blow six guys all one after the other and make them come all under three minutes at Wall Street nightclub. I have no idea if she succeeded or not but the nickname stuck).

He was supposed to be filming with comedy duo French and Saunders the following day and while the BBC car waited outside, Mr. Rivron was drinking mouthwash to try and hide the smell of booze, which we had to send someone out to get.

One night I started chatting to a short but familiar looking man while in Fidenzies. He was obviously someone important as he had a couple of minders with him. He introduced himself as Jimmy, and it was then I realised who he was – champion snooker player Jimmy White.

He really had something – a charm that was hard to resist - and we ended up going back to my place, he wasn't my usual type but we were both coked off our nuts, where we had sex and boy, was Jimmy good. He'd consumed a superhuman amount of booze and Charlie and still was a super performer, he was completely uninhibited.

His minders waited and waited and waited and waited for him in a car outside. They'd call my landline every 30mins then every 2hours to check that everything was okay – he'd always answer no matter what we were up to, usually breathing hard.

We woke up the next day at 11am and Jimmy asked if I'd like come with him to a tournament he had to play somewhere in the Midlands. Polite of him to ask.

"The only catch is we have to go there in a Mini," he said,

"Because of my sponsors."

I was really tempted but I had bookings so, that was that. I had two friends staying with me in the flat at this time – Oliver and Mark. Oliver came into the flat, saw Jimmy, looked at me, and without missing a beat said: "Alright Jimmy, I see you potted the black last night."

*

It was also around this time that I met a very famous neighbour after a night at Fidenzes – Lemmy from Motorhead. His manager had found him a flat just across the way from me and we bumped into each other in the lobby, started talking, went back to his for a drink – he drank nothing but Jack Daniels and took speed. He said he wasn't into coke, that it was much nicer. I beg to differ, but each to their own as the saying goes

"Nah man, it has to be speed!"

He was a big guy, with huge arms covered in scary looking tattoos, a moustache and huge burns. I would have been frightened of him if I'd met him in the street but in person he was sweet and gentle, so different from his public image.

We'd just hang out together, as friends. It was like a release for me – someone I trusted whom I could just be myself around. He wasn't intrusive and never made me feel uncomfortable. I didn't tell him what I did, just that I was trying to become a singer.

I still tried to pursue a singing career and was introduced to record producer Jazz Summers who was once married to Yazz (she had a number one hit with The Only Way Is Up). I travelled to his flat in Belsize Park and even though he had the most terrible acne (he was on a macrobiotic diet which I think had something to do with it), we had sex. I thought if he got what he wanted, this was the way to get a record deal but it wasn't to be. The only thing I got from Jazz was a Christmas card (which I still have) and a book – it was called Living in the Light – one of those personal enlightenment books, which I don't usually go for but I found some of the meditations to be really useful in helping me focus and to be at peace.

I eventually signed up to BMG records ( a one off) and performed as a backing singer for Titiyo – half-sister of Neneh Cherry on a popular TV show called Dance Energy hosted by Normski, who was going out with Janet Street Porter (who later became the editor of the Independent newspaper). We were supposed to mime for the TV show and so I brought one of my girls. She couldn't sing or dance but did shag one of the show's producers. I bumped into Normski in the loos and we ended up having a bit of a snog, more a joke kiss really – just a bit of harmless fun, nothing serious to it at all.

I also recorded my own album and released a single and I remember with pride that I was listed in one magazine - Blues and Soul as one of the notable releases that week – above Mariah Carey. Of course, our careers went in rather different directions (although Mariah did go on to fuck over her record company for a lot of money).

*

'Nigel' found me through What's on and Where to Go Magazine, A wealthy, a sophisticated and intelligent Old Etonian, when I say old, I don't mean in age I mean more that he was steeped in history, and bought up in an era when your word was your bond, not like the likes of David Cameron another Etonian, and his ilk, who while running Britain as Prime Minister seem to be out pure and simply for self-gain, his ancestors had made their fortunes from the slavery trade, he had a lot of issues to work out.

I am a sucker for posh accent and when I met him the first time I was delighted to see he was well-built, tall and handsome man with blonde curly hair.

There's a certain walk all Old Etonians seem to have, a straight-backed stride that exudes confidence and ownership; that they are confident and comfortable in a world made for them.

The only problem as far as I was concerned was that he wasn't the most experienced in bed; but he certainly made up for it in attentiveness he didn't last long and his cock was never, or so it seemed erect to full capacity. I wondered if he was gay as he mentioned he liked men as well.

"So which man would you have sex with if you could have anyone?" I asked.

"I quite fancy ………"

"Not likely that's going to happen."

"It could, he's one of my clients!"

I didn't see him for two or three months after the first time until he called up out of the blue and I saw him again at Abbey Road.

At this time, as I was still trying to get going, I didn't charge much for clients who were quick, like Nigel. He paid £100, which I thought was a good rate, as we'd be done in 30minutes.

"You're beautiful," he told me. "And you're selling yourself short. I'm going to pay you more from now on."

This was a big turning point for me. It made me realise I should have been charging a lot more from day one.

With Nigel our friendship developed to the point where he'd offer to help me out with cash and I called him up for money, £1,000 to pay a certain bill or for a certain out fit for a special occasion or a good holiday.

Nigel also started to hint that he liked kinky stuff; at first he asked to have his nipples squeezed really hard but one day he said: "You know what I really enjoy is domination."

"Well, maybe next time we could experiment."

"Sure."

The next time started very different. I asked him what got him going and he told me to stick my finger up his bottom; so I obliged. "Aaaoow! It's hurting, Madam!"

"Shut the fuck up!"

The moment the domination started, a switch had been thrown in my mind, changing me into someone else. All my normal instincts towards kindness didn't exist anymore. I was in control. Nigel was my bitch now. Perhaps I had a certain 'Maroon mentality', which came out now I had a descendant of the slavers who had fought my ancestors at my mercy.

I didn't have any equipment in my flat at this time, so I was going to have to improvise as best as I could.

"I'm going to put two fingers in." (Covered by a condom)

"Have mercy, have mercy."

"You can beg all you want, you're not getting any mercy, you're here to serve me and that means you're going to take it!"

"Aaaargh!"

Nigel was heavily into amyl nitrate (he also enjoyed rubbing cocaine on various parts of my body. He poured the contents of a bottle onto a cloth and held it over his nose, inhaling it constantly as I tormented him with my two fingers, as the nitrate made his head spin, easing the pain, relaxing his muscles. With my other hand I reached up and grabbed one of his nipples and pinched it hard.

"Madam, I've been so bad, could you shower on me now, and he didn't mean water from the tap."

He loved lying in the bath while I urinated over him – he

would usually come masturbating while I did this.

"Shut up! I'll decide what's next and when."

We stopped once I had had enough. I was in complete control and was exhilarated by the time it was over. After that Nigel and I gradually got more professional but in an ad hoc kind of way in that I learned as I went from each client. I took each thing I learned and would incorporate it with the next client. I loved it when a new client asked for domination as I'd have to find out what their outer limits were and I'd always learn something new.

The next session Nigel suggested I up the pain ante by putting needles through his nipples. I got a lighter, heated the needles, a primitive way of sterilising, and in they went. He screamed like a man on fire but he loved it.

I then had the idea of forcing toothpaste down his penis, then, when I thought he wasn't wincing enough, I had a brainwave. I ran to the kitchen and got some tabasco sauce and added that to the toothpaste. (Clearly a memory stored from my days of old with Christopher Hewitt)

The resulting howl, followed by streams of tears unleashed a feeling of total satisfaction in me.

As we got to know each other more he invited me to his home in a very exclusive part of town, and then to his various other homes.

We snorted lines of coke together. I put some on my nipples and let him suck it off, or sometimes on my pussy. It makes you numb so you can be forever trying to orgasm, if you choose to.

"Natalie, I want you to find me a man," he said one day.

And so I introduced him to Blue, (whose services I would call upon many times in the future for eager clients) a beautifully built black American man, someone I knew I could count on to take an effective part in my domination sessions.

Blue was tall dark, strong and lived as a straight man with a woman in Brixton. She didn't know that he was gay and Blue didn't want to tell her. He said he could fuck her with no problem but he was just not into women. He was, as he put it, 'on the down-low' – a phrase used by American black gay men who live with women.

Once I'd started making a decent amount of money, I moved to Prince of Wales Terrace in Kensington, at the southwest corner of Hyde Park.

In an intimate moment I brought the topic of sexuality up, as our conversation re our sex exploits in the past led to it,

"That friend of yours, he's lying to himself about his sexuality, isn't he?"

"Yes, I'm afraid he is."

"Isn't that what you're doing?"

"It's not the same, I can control it."

Soon after, as I returned home from jogging in Hyde Park, Nigel came to see me.

"My friend died, I'm going to his wake next week, then I'd like to see you for a session afterwards."

My personal thoughts on when someone wants another person to inflict pain on them, is that it's not unlike people that self-harm, and from my limited knowledge, those who self-harm tend to say it's their way of feeling in control, of a given situation.

Maybe that was Nigel' way of controlling his grief,

He arrived for our session in a very sad state. I was sympathetic but at the same time I resented the fact he was using me to offload his misery, or maybe it was more that I was sad for him, and I now had to switch into Mistress mode. I enjoyed our sessions, they were a relief from the day-to-day grind; it was a time when I could get rid of all my tension. So I put that anger to good use and gave poor Nigel a really thorough thrashing that day.

Nigel started to bring props with him – a strap-on-dildo for me, paddles for spanking and chains and collars for restraint. They all came from a specialist gay shop in Earl's Court. Nigel and then other clients would buy me clothes, such as patent leather dresses, leather skirts, collars with studs, PVC boots with six-inch heels, suspenders, stockings, bras, underwear. I found out I could ask them for whatever I wanted and they would find it for me. My clients also brought me a lot of things they liked the look of and I if I wanted anything, I'd tell them and they'd find it for me.

I also knew by now that I was a natural at domination. I'd been a dominant character all my life, so now I decided to advertise my services.

My first domination advert stated: "Strict black lady. Call Brandi for massage."

Brandi was in honour of Brandi Wells, an R&B singer I much admired, well maybe the name more.

Once the ad was in, the men came thick and fast.

Sure, I was doing it for the money, but I chose to do domination because I loved it. From day one, I wanted to do as good a job as possible. I simply had to be the best, plain and simple.

If a man told me I was hurting him I'd say "Good!" I would never stop on his command; I instinctively knew the limits of what I was doing – but there were limits of course and clients nervously enquired if they could use a safe word, which of course they could.

I discovered a particular passion for the cane. There is, I discovered, a certain knack to it. The secret is not to start pounding straight off. Light strokes bring the blood to the surface partly to acclimatise to the pain and to increase the effect of the pain you're about to unleash.

A complaint I often heard from my clients was that other

girls wouldn't go as far as the client wanted. I had no difficulty.

One example was a man who resembled William Hague, but with black hair, well what was left of it.

I met him first, for domination and he loved the cane - badly. He wanted severe caning.

He sprawled bottom up, arms outstretched on the bed below me. I started off lightly, causing the blood to rise and then increased the power of my strokes until welts started to appear. Still he wanted it harder. It got to the point where I was stretching my arm to its full length and twisting with all my strength, as hard as I possibly could onto his rear end. I loved the sound the wood made as it cut through the air, followed by infinitely satisfying gunshot sound as it hit the skin.

The man cried out. Not a yell, a moan, of pain yes, but then deep pleasure. I hadn't tied him to the bed but no matter how hard I hit him, or how often, he did not change position. His skin started to be stripped from his bottom. I started to wonder whether he had a false arse. No normal person could take this amount of caning. If I eased off, he provoked me, making me angry, so I'd hit him harder.

I had no idea what the underlying reason was for his desire to be caned so hard but it was what he wanted more than anything.

After he left that first time, I was tidying up when I noticed a small mark on the wall. I looked more closely and realised it was a perfectly round spot of blood. Then I spotted another just above it – and another – I followed the spatter up the wall and across the ceiling. Tiny specs of blood were everywhere. Now I'd have to get the decorators in, and next time I was going to wear a big pair of shades.

He later bought me a fresh cane after mine lost its bendiness and paid well for my services and – knowing he was extremely wealthy - I eventually tripled my fee – it was hard for this type of client to find someone like me, as willing as I was to go as far as he wanted.

There was only one other girl I found – who went on to become a university professor – who could give him as good a seeing-to as I did. She had really strong arms (I wondered for a while whether she was transsexual but she fell pregnant and named her baby after me) and my cane lover never complained that she wasn't beating him hard enough.

One of my girls, Yvonne, met him at a party I gave and they ended up living together. This was not uncommon. After all, if the client and the girl understood each other's mind and sexual needs – humanity's primary driving force - everything else pretty much follows in its wake.

*

I discovered that clients into S&M were quite different from clients into straight sex. They tended to be extremely loyal. Although they came in all shapes and sizes and although many of them were not at all attractive physically, (although there were from time to time some lovely young bucks who passed through, city boys full of stress and cash, over flowing with cash from their huge wage bonuses) they knew how to play the role of a slave and some were prepared to go to extreme lengths to fulfil their desires.

Robin was one of the first clients, after Nigel, who saw me for many years. Things did not get off to a good start, however. He made the mistake of arriving twenty minutes too early.

"You're way too early," I told him crossly.

"Can I come back later?" he answered meekly.

"If you want," and I slammed the door in his face.

I didn't like the look of him. He was middle-aged, shabbily

dressed and didn't seem sophisticated. One should never judge a book by its cover of course, but I couldn't help myself when it came to my work.

I was rather hoping Robin wouldn't come back but when he did I let him in and demanded a higher fee, hoping he wouldn't have enough cash. He remained undeterred and produced the money.

He was 5' 7" with pure white, thinning hair and a stocky bulldog body. He had a hard big belly and solid, very thick long legs (he skied a lot). Robin liked to have the nipple clamps put on immediately, as soon as he'd removed his shirt. Once they were on, Robin liked to start by massaging me (he'd bring all kinds of scented exotic oil for this purpose) during which time we'd discuss what we were going to do during the session.

During one massage Robin said: "Your indifference when you refused to let me in that first day was intoxicating. I knew straight away you were the perfect Mistress."

One of his favourite acts on him involved a strap-on dildo. Another favourite game of his was to parade around on all fours like a puppy, wearing a dog collar while I caned and whipped him.

Robin had a high pain threshold (thanks in part to coke) and our sessions grew longer and longer. I even branded him on the inside of his thigh using a hot fork. Once the burn had faded I'd apply another one – it was a way of saying that Robin always belonged to me, even when he was out in the 'real' world.

Although Robin became a loyal slave, I never would have thought that I'd still be seeing him 15 years down the line.

Once the session started, roles were maintained until the end – there was no small talk or dialogue that wasn't in the context of our session – and we reverted back to our 'other selves' afterwards and chatted.

If you want to be dominated by me then you're going to get it good and proper. If you're going to be a wimp, then don't ask me to dominate you – it's a fantasy yes, but it must be taken seriously, strict rules in place so that no mistakes are made. Most girls couldn't do it – they could only 'act' like a dominatrix, they were unable to do it instinctively, but if it's not your thing it's never going to be a convincing role play for the client. Luckily, as business started to take off, I did manage to find enough girls prepared to go the extra mile with a client.

Most men didn't even check their injuries after the session was over. For them, the experience with me was exhilarating, like jumping into an ice pool – it's not exactly pleasant at the time but afterwards your skin tingles and your whole body hums with life. My men always left my home with a spring in their step.

I had the feeling I was teaching them something about what was physically possible, what their outer limits were.

Me in my zone

# Thirteen

# SLEEPING BEAUTY

'Richard', a big-shot who lived in Chelsea, was married with children. He'd divorced his wife who'd since got mixed up with cocaine barons in South America where she had been imprisoned at some point. Richard was trying to get her out. "One can't let the mother of one's children perish in jail," he told me in his public school accent.

He resided between New York and London, I really liked Richard, he was a charming English gent, middle-aged and generous, had a big nose and small beady eyes, I loved his laugh it was like a squeaky mouse, he too enjoyed the obligatory corduroy trousers, the uniform of the upper class Chelsea gent. We called him Mr. Squasher because he really liked to feel the pressure. He wasn't into sex, nor men, he was into being squashed, for the main part.

I once watched as six naked 20-something girls sat on Richard, who was high on ecstasy and coke, while he wheezed below their bottoms, fighting for breath.

When I didn't have enough girls available, Richard would visit me at home. I kept my home address secret from some of my girls; I wanted my privacy and if any of them got into trouble for whatever reason, I wanted them to call me, rather than show up at my door. Most times our session would just be me and him alone, other times he'd request a few girls to join us.

He was at his happiest when he was being squashed, the heavier the ladies the happier he was quite an easy booking, but a tad boring.

Richard did however delight in pleasuring the girls and me with his tongue, which did take away the boredom for a while.

Sitting on someone for endless hours and squashing them while getting paid, should have been nothing to moan about, all considered.

Richard liked to do Amyl Nitrate (no surprise there), ecstasy and coke. Usually, once we were in slave/Mistress roles, I'd start by turning him into a table. He'd get on all fours; I'd rest my feet on him and then start putting glasses or whatever object I felt inclined to balance on him.

"Anything drops and you're going to get it."

So, 4 or 5 or more of us would pile on top of gentle Richard, whoever was first on top of Richard had to be extra careful they didn't bear the brunt of the other girls weight either, we would writhe on him, applying as much pressure with our bodies, I must admit apart from your young ravers, I'd never come across anyone that could take as many Ecstasy tablets as he did, up to 6 on occasions.

One night, when I was with Mr. Squasher, a friend of mine called.

"Come on Natalie, let's go to Stringfellows, I need to let my hair down and party."

"I can't, I'm with Mr. Squasher."

But I was tempted. I'd got model passes for the agency back in the day, which meant we were whisked inside past any queue and, once inside, there were always plenty of confident and wealthy men up for a good time. I thought for a moment; then had an evil little idea.

I turned Squasher into a table and waited until he

moved and dropped something.

"That's it, you useless piece of shit! Now I'm going to punish you."

"Yes Mistress!"

I went into my cupboard of tricks and came back with handcuffs – with a proper lock. I fastened his wrists around a radiator and left the house.

When I rolled up to Stringfellows my friend asked me what happened to Mr. Squasher.

"Oh him, he's back at my flat, chained up, awaiting my return."

"You're terrible!"

"He's getting what he wants and I'm getting what I want, so what's the problem?"

And it was true; when I finally returned he was quite happy with his evening, as was I.

I was so knackered and very inebriated, I removed the hand cuffs, poured out a glass of champers, and laid on top of him.

At some point, I heard a whimpering voice, 'Natalie darling, I really need to go now'

'Uh! What?

'It's 8am'

As I tried to get my baring, I realised, oh no! I'd fallen asleep on top of Richard and he must have been too polite to wake me.

I didn't charge any extra money, for the overtime, although it crossed my mind.

## Fourteen

# A TORY WHIP

I ran Black Beauties alongside my domination business. This was 1991, and although the economy was deep in recession, Black Beauties was doing so well that I turned down more girls than I took on – only the classiest made it on to my books.

In the beginning I let clients get away with too much. I never liked it when they tried to turn our relationship into something resembling girlfriend/boyfriend. The worst ones were the clients who wanted to get their money's worth. They'd stretch it out for too long:

"I don't want to come just yet, I want to do something to you."

It was okay if they were paying me enough – anyone forking out £2,000 a session was welcome to hang around, as long as I didn't have another client waiting.

The £300-ers had to be quick. And as for clients such as Patrick a Priest, I disposed of them as soon as the agency had taken off.

At the same time, I was always turned on by new clients not in a sexual way although there were exceptions and looked forward to our journey together, finding out what made them tick, similar to when you meet someone in `normal ` circumstances you want to impress and it's all about the anticipation. I'd get the biggest rush when the public school types came for their first session – I liked their indifference and aloofness. They always knew exactly what they wanted, weren't afraid to ask and didn't drag things out – and more often than not I'd blow their minds along the way, breaking their thick upper crust veneer.

Part of my success came from treating my girls well and trusting them – I loaned them money if they were short and they worked hard for me in return. I ended up with fifty girls in total, twenty worked most days. I ran everything myself and used a private second line where regulars could leave a name and number or hotel room and a time.

I had come a long way from that 14-year-old girl, freezing and homeless at the bus stop. Now I lived in Kensington, bought brand new cars, designer clothes and had dozens of men in the palm in the hand – I could have anyone I wanted.

The client list – for domination and straight sex - grew and grew, so much so that I became picky. If the caller didn't sound well educated or wealthy, then I wouldn't go. If I didn't like the look of where they lived or the client's appearance, I'd turn around and leave.

For example, I was once booked to come to a flat in Cadogan Gardens at 2-3am. I'd always have the cab wait until the door closed behind me. In this case, when the huge black door opened, there was no light behind it, only total darkness inside. Even though it was a good address, a chill passed through my body. I could just make out a young man in the gloom behind the door. He stepped forward slightly, and I could see he was probably in his mid-twenties.

"Oh hello," I said, "Hold on a moment, I'm just going to pay my cab."

When I got back to the cab I told him to take me home. He was probably harmless but when my gut told me to leave, I always listened.

I usually asked new clients a few searching questions – If I didn't like the sound of someone over the phone, I wouldn't see them but if I did, then it was a roller coaster for all concerned.

Sometimes my judgement was off, as in the case of 'Stephen' who spoke with a bit of a cockney accent. So, as he didn't sound posh enough for me, I gave the booking to June.

I decided to take over after she returned alive and unharmed and sang Stephen's praises, mentioning he was also exceedingly wealthy to boot. He turned out to be a global player in the publishing world and was one of the few clients whom I almost ended up falling for.

Stephen quickly fell for me in a big way and booked me all the time; he was into swinging and took me with him to Paris, to a secret, exclusive and expensive club (the annual membership was several thousand pounds) called Cleopatra. Everyone there seemed to be completely respectable, well-heeled and with reputable careers.

I found the whole thing a bit seedy. Personally, I couldn't see the logic in it – why have random sex for no reason, i.e., if you're not getting paid? I preferred being with my clients, who were wealthy and wonderful and had the most extraordinary predilections.

At one end of the club was a pitch-dark area where strangers were snogging and touching one another. If someone touched you when you were walking around and you didn't want to do anything all you had to do was say 'non' and they'd leave you alone. It was all very civilised.

If you said 'oui' and then after a bit of a fondle you both decided to fuck then you could go to a separate room.

I went into one room to see what was going on and

there was a young woman on a makeshift bench with a cock in her mouth, another in her fanny and was wanking two men on either side of her. I'm in the business and this to me was more disturbing than anything. I felt as though the women who were there did it to please their husbands. The room stank of sweat and sex – not in a good way – and the noises, grunting men and moaning women was unnerving, I hated it.

We didn't fuck anyone - even each other - in the club. Stephen always said if I didn't want to he wouldn't expect it and he wouldn't do anything either, although I felt he would have indulged had he been alone as he regularly frequented those type of places.

I was briefly tempted by a really good looking young guy, has I was wondering around the joint, this guy which under any other circumstances I would have happily dated, tugged my at my harm, I was pretty much caught off guard – Stephen was off somewhere else - so I decided to kiss him – but he tasted of another woman's pussy, a total turn-off. I stopped immediately made my excuse and went searching for Stephen. Stephen also took me to an even more exclusive get-together in a huge chateau about 45minutes outside of Paris. We drove through huge electronic gates into expansive grounds late evening.

This swingers club was for judges, lawyers and politicians - nobody could become a member without being recommended by another member and then going through a thorough vetting by the club.

Members, who were sworn to secrecy, could bring a guest but they then had to take responsibility for the way they behaved. Anything against the rules and you were immediately blackballed.

The evening started with a fancy lobster and scallop dinner over one long table. I love lobster and scallops but I could barely touch my food, as I was so apprehensive about what was going to happen. Finished, we were given a locker key and everyone got changed into togas, leaving our clothes and belongings in the lockers.

Then it was time to 'mix'; you simply said 'oui' or 'non' when someone touched you. Soon, everywhere you turned, people were having sex.

"If you want to do anything, go ahead," Stephen said.

"Are you going to?" I asked.

"We'll see."

But he said if I wasn't going to swing then neither would he. So we returned to our hotel, got undressed and climbed into bed.

"We have a great time together, don't we?" I asked.

"Yes."

"So how come you're into swinging?"

"I just find it easier to have sex with strangers than someone I know."

"But you know me... Don't you?"

We started having sex and I don't know if it was the fact we were in Paris, had a view of the Eiffel Tower or whether the brandy I had drunk from the minibar had gone to my head, but something odd happened. There was an intense moment of closeness, perhaps the purity of doing it alone, privately after the seediness of seeing all those other people. Perhaps our experience and conversation had made Stephen open himself to the intense pleasure and trust that's possible with someone you know well, when you truly give yourself to one another, and I responded to that – it was wonderful.

Afterwards, Stephen said: "I think I'm falling in love with you."

I almost said it back to him. Not quite, but almost.

At the other end of the posh-voice scale was Nicholas

Villiers I decided to see him as soon as he gave me his address – was a lovely street in Belgravia, one of London's most expensive areas.

Nicholas was in banking, (no surprise given the address) he was very well connected in both society and celebrity worlds) quickly became a regular and over time he asked me to bring other girls - for us both to enjoy. Although I felt as though I was still in my prime, Vincent liked his girls as young as possible. This was fine with me as I didn't enjoy sex with Vincent (we just weren't compatible; he spent ages licking my pussy and wasn't very good at it) but I enjoyed his company. He had a dry sense of humour and I liked his deep thick gravelly educated accent, deepened by the expensive cigars he loved to smoke.

Nicholas liked some domination, but what he took in abuse he gave back in upper-class arrogance. He loved to see Peggy and Carol whenever possible, especially Peggy, as she wasn't worried about not using a condom and Vincent liked that. He was obviously extremely wealthy and so I doubled my usual price for whatever he wanted and he never hesitated in accepting.

His house was cluttered with antiques of all kinds but an oil painting of a young Indian boy really stood out amongst his over crowed home of antiques. It was clearly old and the almost reluctant look on the young boys face caught my curiosity, I was very curious about this piece.

I was at Fidenzes, the Mayfair nightclub, when I met a young Filipino girl who told me she had once been a man. She looked so feminine, so beautiful that I couldn't believe her and I asked if she wouldn't mind showing me the results of the operation.

She was happy to do so, in the ladies' loos. It looked good, although the slit was much higher than a woman's normally is. I told her about Nicholas and she agreed to see him. I couldn't wait to introduce her – she would be the jewel in the crown.

Sure enough, Nicholas' eyes practically popped out of his head; he loved the fact she had once been a he. Nicholas stayed with her for a long time – and then tried to see her behind my back, but she was honest and always paid my commission, even after Nicholas started contacting her directly.

There's an ideal sexual partner out there for all of us; unfortunately most people aren't lucky enough to find them in the random flux of life; most of the time we don't even know what we're looking for. But if you have expert help, like me, your chances of success are dramatically increased

Nicholas was a well-connected individual a socialite high in society, one evening he called me up requesting 2 ladies for his evening's entertainment, nothing would have been unusual in his request, but tonight it was a little different. He had a pal 'George' round and he wanted a lady also.

My girls had all been booked out, and one of them was Carol, there was a Conference on in Earls Court, when there's a conference in town most agencies are busy and so I was pretty thin on the ground with someone for Nicholas' taste and requirements, I couldn't just send any old thing, he was a good regular and when you went to see him boy! did you have to work for your dollars. Long gone were the days that he desired me, yep I'd once been his flavour of the month, I was only too happy to have been relegated, 'cause when you entered his domain you didn't leave till he'd fucked you into the ground. Nicholas was quite keen on Carol she was becoming his little favourite, but I'd seen It all before, eventually it wears out, and it's "do you have anyone new Natalie?" but for now she was flavour of the month.

Carol had also fallen for Nicholas on a personal level, I think it was is upper class arrogance that swung it, she liked men like that, and with her cold as ice attitude, they suited each other.

I called her to check when she would be free, and the professional that she is, she soon called to say she was free, Nicholas had requested some cocaine, I had to call my dealer and get it to him on time for when the girls arrived. I was out of luck that day, as I couldn't get another girl in time, but Nicholas just didn't just use my agency, and so he got another girl from somewhere else, later that night I got a call from carol, she was as excited as a young puppy with a toy. "You will not believe who this 'George' is?" "Who Carol," I replied in a curt manner, then she said the name of Mr Charmer himself, "It's Nigel Havers, the actor", "really!" I said, "yes and I'm with him."

"So he's George"

"Yes",

"Where are you? Can he hear you?"

"No I'm in the loo",

"No way, put him on the phone."

She went to the bed room.

"My friend wants to speak to you, can I put her on?"

A few seconds later he said; "Hi, it's George".

The next time Nicholas called me for two girls for him and Nigel

I said to him "oh, so George is Nigel hey," he replied back with shh!

I made a point this time that I would deliver the coke, it wasn't unusual for me to pop it round to Nicholas if I had the time, I made sure I did.

On this particular night, as luck would have it, I didn't

have 2 black girls to fit the bill, I only had Carol around, all the other girls left wouldn't have suited, Nicholas was very particular in the height, complexion, breast size, no more than a size 10, and did cocaine he was a pain at times, but a very good payer, I asked Nicholas if it was ok to send a white girl instead, Nigel didn't mind.

So Carol went over and a blonde girl called Debbie, a bit past her sell by date, but I kept my fingers cross.

Off I darted over to Belgravia to deliver the Charlie, I wasn't going to miss out on meeting up with the star of Oscar-winning epics, once he had a line up his nose, however, he would harp on about the past and injustices in the world. He was lovely, but very melancholic.

He started going on and on about the coal miners and how hard done by they were, about how Thatcher had screwed Britain and so on. He had this real injustice mind set, I didn't stay too long as Nicholas needed to get on with his planned night of debauchery with Nigel and the girls.

I asked Debbie how it had all went, she said Nigel hadn't been able to perform.

"I think it was too much coke" she said "once he had a line he couldn't preform."

Carol told me a different story "He just didn't fancy her in the least."

"So what happened"?

"Once he'd had a few lines, and you know how it can make someone talk too much? Well he talked so much that Debbie fell asleep."

Poor Nigel, if I'd been with him, he'd have had no time to talk, that's for sure.

*

One well-spoken man called Black Beauties to ask about 'procuring a lady for a home visit.' Not all my girls could offer this as many lived double lives but as I was living across the road from Kensington Palace in a gorgeous duplex, Prince of Wales Terrace, I could see clients there.

Forty-five minutes later, David (a Conservative member of Parliament although I was unaware at the time) in his mid-40s arrived wearing a Burberry mac at my door, holding a bottle of champagne. I wasn't physically attracted to him but he laid on the charm, telling me I was much prettier than I'd sounded on the phone, and I just love a complement. It was always important to find something that attracted me to a client. I wanted to be the best they ever had and so it was important to find something in them that I liked.

I asked what he did for living.

"Breast surgeon."

Sometime in our session as it was going free and I'd never had before, I asked him if he'd mind examining my breasts, which he did, looking back he must have been mortified as he wasn't really a flipping breast surgeon in the first place! At some point after I'd given him a massage, he explained that he had issues with obtaining an erection and promptly then opened his ministerial briefcase and produced a cock-pump, a contraption that helped him rise to the occasion. I'd never clapped eyes on one before, a man who clearly desires sex should do what works for him. He was embarrassed at first but I was able to make him feel relaxed about it.

He became a regular. We'd go into my black and grey marble bathroom with wall-to-wall mirrors. I'd strip and he'd pour baby oil all over me. Once I was totally dripping, I'd stand in front of him, my back pressed against him, and writhe as we watched our reflections.

"You are a beautiful goddess, your skin is so silky," he'd say.

He liked lots of dirty sex talk as I pumped his cock to reach erection. "What a lovely juicy hard cock. Do you want to fuck this black pussy?"

Once he was erect he'd slide a cock ring onto the base of his penis to ensure he stayed hard. He was kind and caring but tried a little too hard. I prefer a man to be more aloof but he paid well, treated me with respect and bought me presents, such as Chanel no 5, after I mentioned I liked it.

It wasn't until much later – after I saw him on television - that I found out he was in fact in the conservative cabinet, David Maclean now an EX-Conservative minister and TORY CHIEF WHIP, LORD BLENCATHRA and that he kept his cock pump in his ministerial briefcase.

Most of my clients were high profile businessmen on tight schedules: 5pm meeting, 6pm hooker, 7pm business dinner. If a man arrives at an evening business meeting freshly showered, then you know what he's been up to.

Sometimes David' schedule meant I had to squeeze him between other appointments but his 'requirements' often meant me taking more time than I would have liked.

One evening, this happened with one of my favourites, John, Eton educated, who was one of the topmost executives at Lloyds of London – he (along with other execs I've come across) ran Lloyds while high on coke and crack.

On this occasion David' pump wasn't having the desired effect.

"What's on your mind?"

"Stressful Cabinet meeting."

The look on his face told me he'd not meant for that to slip – this was when I first realised my client was a Cabinet minister.

I pretended not to hear and continued pumping away!

John was due any moment so, frustrated, I slapped the Minister's arse and said: "Come on, get that fucking cock hard or I'll spank you much harder."

This had an effect.

"Do it again," he said, "That's more like it."

"So that's what you like. Why didn't you say so sooner? On your knees." with some urgency

He followed my orders like a hungry pup.

Then the buzzer went. Leaving David to his pump I went to let in John who was extremely eager to get started and could barely control his excitement. John was of slight build, scrawny plus the cocaine was taking its toll on him, about 5ft 8" and with really spindly legs, strawberry blond greying hair. For some reason, he reminded me of a character from Monty Python in his behaviour, very animated and eccentric, I explained the situation as I led him to the lounge. John was curious about my mystery client. I told him to wait, so he put on a video he'd brought with him, of which he had a stock pile of, he was friends, with Lord 'A', this was from the Lord's collection and was very hardcore, even for me, though I have to confess I've never seen the point of porn.

In no time at all I was running back and forth between the Pump Action Minister and the masturbating Executive. All I needed now was the gas meter reader to arrive… David finished first and I managed to sneak him out the fire exit without John intervening.

When I told John I'd been tempted to let their paths cross, I eagerly told him about the fact that the other client was a minister.

For some reason, a disproportionate number of my clients were old Etonians. Even today, when someone mentions they've gone to Eton, I immediately look at them in a different light. I would also go on to discover that there were plenty more parliamentarians who were keen on domination.

John came across as a very seasoned client from the first time we met. He was overly familiar which was unusual; clients tended to be distant to start with and warmed up over time. John was confident and kept no secrets from me from the start, telling me what he did for a living, where he worked, and even gave me his office number in case I needed to reach him. He chatted freely about work and social events while we listened to Rossini and drank Charles Heidsieck champagne.

I liked to keep the Mistress/slave relationship as real as possible and that usually meant maintaining a distance but, as John was so good at slotting into the submissive role, I was able to work with him and I wanted to make all of his fantasies come true.

At the start of each session, I made John go to the bathroom and change into a costume of my choice. Sometimes it was dog collar and rubber pants, sometimes fishnet stockings with suspenders and a bra but every now and then John would come with something in mind, already in his briefcase. He also carried nipple clamps, handcuffs and a leather paddle. I supplied my own cane, as this was not something he could hide in his briefcase. Sometimes he even brought some of his wife's stockings and suspenders.

Many wives knew what their husbands got up to and put up with it, thanks to family trust funds and the associated lifestyles, not to mention their families' reputations. 'After all,' I'm sure they said to themselves, 'What threat can a whore be to me?' Well, their husbands trusted me with their lives and did things with me they would never tell another soul about.

On the night I made John's ultimate fantasy come true, he had brought his own pair of rubber pants, a black leather silver-studded dog collar and lead. The rubber pants kept bruising to minimum, and he loved the feeling of them on his skin.

John had been left reeling by Black Wednesday and even though his position at Lloyds (and his fortune) was safe, he'd nonetheless decided to sell his David Hockney collection to top-up his cash flow.

The recession never had an effect on my trade and I never dropped my prices. Many of my clients were millionaires who could not be hurt by any recession but others came to me even when cash was low, for an escape, to release innumerable tensions and for the relief of relinquishing control over their destinies for a few precious hours – this was what they were addicted to.

Once John had changed, he liked to take a few lines of coke, so after snorting lines chopped out on his personal coke mirror, he was ready for whatever I, his Mistress demanded. From this moment he could only address me as Mistress and be my unquestioning slave until I decreed the session was over.

"On your knees, you little shit, do it now and don't rile me." I spoke with command that could not be questioned.

I held a paddle in my hand. I stroked it across his face, softly at first; then gently started to tap him.

"What are you going to do for your Queen today slave?"

"Whatever you desire my beautiful Black Goddess."

His eyes shone with excitement.

"Get on all fours and walk like the dog you are, until I tell you to stop."

He obeyed and crawled along the floor, pushing his ass up at me, eagerly expecting a spanking.

"Stop! Crawl over to the radiator and stay there, with

your back facing me. I am going to give you the thrashing of a lifetime."

"Yes Mistress. I wouldn't dare disobey you Mistress you know that, don't you?"

"Did I ask you to speak, you little turd?"

"No Mistress, you didn't, please forgive me."

I stepped forward and, with my weight behind me, gave him two whacks on his bottom. Then I slowly peeled his rubber pants down and gave him a dozen slaps on each cheek, starting gently but building up harder and harder, getting the blood to rise before reaching a crescendo and letting him have six brutally hard whacks on each cheek, forcing him to cry out.

"Don't fucking wince, or I'll use my cane. You don't want that do you?"

"I will take whatever punishment you feel I deserve my Queen."

"Little slave boy, lie flat on the ground. What do you think your mistress has in mind for you now"?

"I don't know."

I handcuffed both of his hands to the legs of the radiator.

John, a powerful man who controlled billions of pounds, a man who could affect the British economy for good or ill, was now spread-eagled before me, face down and unable to move.

I walked over to the sofa, sat down and poured a glass of champagne before lighting a cigarette. I had a surprise for John. We had discussed this 'little surprise' after our last session, but he didn't know he was going to get it so soon.

"Slave boy."

"Yes Mistress."

"A surprise is on its way."

I looked at my Cartier watch, bought for me by an English banker based in Hong Kong, It would be here in ten minutes.

"Do you remember you told me about a fantasy you had, about a large black cock up your ass?"

"Yes I do Mistress."

"Well, tonight's the night."

"What do you mean Mistress?"

"Don't make me say it again, slave boy. You are going to be buggered today. Now listen very carefully Slave. Do not disappoint me. You will do whatever I ask. You will be the most perfect Slave. Do you understand?"

"Yes Mistress. May I ask a question?"

"You may."

"What does he look like?"

"A black, 6ft 3 American with a nine-inch cock." This was Blue.

"Can you take off my handcuffs before he arrives Mistress? I would like to kiss his feet when I greet him."

I smiled. Was John feeling vulnerable down there? If so, then good.

"No. You will only kiss my feet and both of you will do what I say."

John wouldn't be able to see Blue when he arrived. That was just the way I wanted it, building the intensity and anticipation.

The intercom rang right on time and I buzzed Blue in. He was extremely handsome and butch, with black skin as smooth as silk.

"Hi John, how are you doing?" he asked, his baritone causing John to shiver.

John's reply was barely above a whisper.

"Excited."

Blue snorted four lines of coke.

"I hope that won't affect the hardness of your erection," I said.

"Don't worry, nothing is going to stop me from fucking that sweet white ass."

Blue went to the bathroom to change and returned wearing nothing but a silver studded black leather jock strap, his ass exposed and glistening with oil.

I started to instruct Blue to go over to John and massage his ass, but it was clear he did not want to waste any time because he'd already straddled John before I could complete my sentence.

He started to squeeze and slap John's ass and then ran his tongue up and down John' back, slowly and lightly.

"Oh Mistress," John begged, "May I please be released so I can see my Black Master?"

"No!"

John was in ecstasy. I'd asked Blue to use his initiative, so I let him carry on.

"That's enough for now," I commanded. "Blue, take his handcuffs off."

I handed Blue the keys and he released John.

John turned over and gasped when he saw Blue's face for the first time. They started to kiss, and were soon in a passionate embrace, Blue tugging at John's hair and pulling him close at the same time.

"That's enough, I can see we're going to have some fun tonight."

I handed John the mirror with the coke and told him to snort two huge lines. This done, I told Blue to get on his knees.

"Slave, go over to Blue and play with his cock."

"Oh yes Mistress."

They were both on their knees as John started to stroke Blue's cock. It quickly grew until it looked ready to burst, I watched, fascinated, as his thick veins pulsated.

"Put it in your mouth, slave."

"Blue, you better not come," I demanded.

"Don't be alarmed," he replied. "I can come all over his face and in his mouth and still get hard again, if you want."

"Not yet."

I walked over to John and screwed on adjustable nipple clamps until he yelped.

"Mistress, please have mercy!"

I slapped him across his face. "Shut up slave. There is no pleasure without pain."

John moaned and muttered 'Thank you Mistress,' over and over.

I then fetched the amyl nitrate. John liked to use this when on the verge of orgasm, but it was for the both of them now, I can't stand the smell but most of my slaves loved it.

I screwed the nipple clamps as tight as they would go but by this time the Amyl had taken John to another plane. His eyes were bloodshot red; his hand was a blur as he wanked himself with increasing urgency while Blue grunted, pounded and thrusted as deep as he could. Suddenly Blue took his cock out, threw off the condom off and exploded all over John's body. I couldn't believe how much there was; I'd never seen so much come out of one man. John rubbed it over his body and hungrily licked his fingers.

"You enjoyed yourself didn't you Blue?" I asked.

"Oh yes indeed."

He then went to the bathroom, got changed and came back into the lounge. I paid him his £250 fee, he said goodbye and I let him out.

I then looked down at John.

"How was that, slave boy?"

"A bit on the painful side", he replied, forgetting for a moment that we were still in session before hastily adding, "But I'm certainly not complaining, Mistress."

"Now come here and pleasure your Mistress."

"Oh of course Mistress, what do you bid me?"

"Get on your knees and lick my heels."

He started licking one of my 6-inch heels. I gently stuck it into his mouth. He stared directly into my eyes as he sucked hard on them.

"Good slave, good boy, now move over to my other heel."

He ended up polishing my whole shoe with his tongue.

"You can't have all this pleasure without a sacrifice," I said, reaching for my cane.

"Kneel on all fours." I slashed and whipped until I lost count of the number of strokes that had left red criss-cross patterned welts across his cheeks.

He took it all with typical British stoicism but every now and then he let out a wince, and that made me hit him harder, aiming with military precision; it excited me to show no mercy.

"Thank you Mistress, I belong only to you."

This pleased me so I decided to allow John to come.

"You now have my permission to play with your cock until you release that pathetic and worthless sperm that no one wants."

"Thank you Mistress!"

John raised his head slightly while I held the opened brown bottle of Amyl to his nose. He inhaled long and hard.

"Who wants that useless little cock, you perverted little shit?" I shouted. "Your Mistress commands you to come now. You don't know how lucky you are that I allow you so much pleasure."

"Oh, oh, I do my Queen," he whimpered.

I poured baby oil over his hand and his penis and he jerked his hand at high speed.

I spat in his face. "Come now, you useless worm, with your worthless shrivelled cock."

"Yes Mistress, yes" he said urgently, letting out a huge, long groan that became a scream as he came, jerking and twitching with every spasm until he fell back on the floor and lay there, still, utterly, utterly exhausted.

## Fifteen

# KLAUS

Another day, another new client. I threw open the door to find a short man with a neat haircut and a small moustache standing in front of me.

"Good day," he said in a German accent. "I believe I have an appointment."

For once I was lost for words. He looked a little - no – he looked a lot like Adolf Hitler he had the same haircut and side parting, unbelievably, the same little moustache.

"My name is Klaus Danner" he offered. "We spoke on the phone."

I regained my composure. "Yes, of course, come in."

Minutes later, I was pushing down with all my strength, suffocating Klaus – who was tied to the bed – me with a pillow over his face. This wasn't because I wanted to kill the little Hitler lookalike; he was just into suffocation.

One of his pink, plump little arms started banging weakly on the bed, signalling he was on the verge of passing out. I lifted the pillow; he sucked in a breath and his eyes rolled forwards into their sockets and focused on me, a look of complete contentment on his face.

Suffocating a client always made me a bit nervous. We all know that erotic asphyxiation is not something to be tried on one's own (see for example the obituaries of actor

David Carradine, MP Stephen Milligan and - most likely - the rock star Michael Hutchence) but even with someone there to watch over you, it's still pretty high-risk. Klaus who was also in the banking field, seemed pretty clued up, so I went along with him.

I wasn't all that experienced in this particular field and apart from keeping my wits about me, I somewhat let him coach me.

My anxiety was high, I wanted him to get his money's worth but at the same time I didn't want to go on trial for manslaughter!

I saw Klaus every time he came over to England, each time I saw him he pushed his thrill even further, he too liked to use Amyl Nitrate, the routine usually was that he'd inhale the vapour from the bottle of Amyl and I would then put a pillow over his face, that wasn't sufficient for him, oh no! he now had progressed to having me pour the Amyl straight onto cotton wool and then sticking it up his nostrils and then placing the pillow over his face, this was highly dangerous and I realised that I literally had his life in my hands which was the whole point of the exercise, I think sub consciously there is a part in the individual that wants to die or come close to.

On this particular day,

As he was leaving, he asked: "Do you undertake commissions abroad?"

"For the right price."

"I want you to come to Germany and meet me at a particular hotel."

He handed me a card of the hotel and another one, with a picture of a woman on it.

"This is what I want you to wear when you come down to join me for dinner."

"You've got to be joking."

"I will pay you £5,000."

"Deutschland here I come."

*

I pulled up in a taxi outside the luxury hotel, deep in Germany's Black Forest. It was a beautiful spot; a rushing river curved past the hotel and rich green trees crowded the hills, behind which, in the distance, were snow-capped mountains.

I was to meet him for dinner in the old mill – converted into a luxury restaurant. I made my way to the room, got changed, looked at myself in the mirror, thought 'I can't believe I'm here and about to do this,' reminded myself of the £5,000 Klaus had paid me, took a deep breath and marched out the door and into the hotel.

There was only one way to play this, in character, as a performance. I could not smile or look uncertain, otherwise someone would question me. I had to let people know by the way I walked that to question me would be to question death.

People looked three times – twice because they couldn't believe what they'd seen the first time and the third time because my outfit simply required more study – and it was unlikely they were going to see something like this again in their lifetime. Most of the clientele seemed to be elderly, retired businessmen and their wives in suits and smart conservative outfits - I think most of them had rarely even been in the presence of a black girl before - so I really stood out.

I was wearing patent leather 6-inch heels, fishnet stockings and a skin-tight patent leather dress with two silver zips all the way down from top to bottom, one on the front, the other on the back. I couldn't zip the dress all the way down in the back without turning my walk into a hobble – so I left the zip half way up at the back, exposing my fishnets and suspenders. It hugged my ass so tightly I might as well have not been wearing it all. Men's shocked gazes took in everything, disappearing down my cleavage and between my legs; women looked both disgusted and terrified.

I entered the restaurant. Klaus stood up and beckoned me over with a smile. The maître d' looked like he was not going to recover the power of speech anytime soon.

As I sat down, I could see that Klaus was pleased about the extreme reaction I was causing – he was aroused in fact. And that was at the root of his fantasy, why he looked like Hitler – Klaus loved to shock.

He picked up the menu. "What would you like?"

What followed was a perfectly ordinary dinner, brightened when one waiter, studying me when he should have been looking where he was going, raised his hand to push the swing door and instead shoved the face of the maître d' coming the other way.

Some diners left after only spotting us once they'd taken their seats, muttering under their breath, while others stayed for the entire meal, perhaps wondering what the Führer was doing in this hotel with a black dominatrix.

Klaus paid the bill and we left, bound for his room, where he spent most of the night with a pillow over his face before passing out (with exhaustion) and then snoring like a baby for the rest of the night.

Klaus was not one of my favourites, but he paid well. I could tell he was the sort of man to whom nobody ever paid attention – and a small man complex. The reason he was such a successful banker was because he was so prudent – he never took a risk at work. So, while in the real world he was a conservative nobody, in my realm he was the most powerful, frightening man the globe had ever seen, a man who loved to shock and who lived for danger.

Klaus had another Mistress in Germany, at some point things started to unravel in his life, he mentioned that he had somehow got himself into bad situation with her, that she had financially, got the better of him, blackmail? I wondered to myself, the last time Klaus tried to pay me, his cheque bounced. I didn't chase Klaus for it, I felt sorry for him, and never saw him again.

## Sixteen

# SMALL BONE

The men I saw that were into domination, were at times extremely reckless given their rank in life, and were totally addicted just like other people are to drugs and alcohol. Which meant they were often addicted to me. It's not easy to find a good dominatrix, let alone one whom you can trust with your life. Many years back when domination was more of a dirty secret not as widely out in the open as it is today, it was nearly impossible.

Sometimes the addiction took over and the men just didn't have boundaries any more, they'd lose sense of reality. After all, no normal human being would allow himself to be whipped and buggered while taking drugs, while his 90-something mother was dying upstairs.

Clients fell for me for all sorts of reasons but I discovered that the easiest way to ensure a client became a regular returner was - after giving them the performance of their life on the first meeting - to make it hard work for them to see me, and that meant making sure they knew I wasn't desperate to see them – at all.

When they called I'd say something like: "Can I see you? Well, not on the day you want to see me."

I wasn't even doing this for effect; it was a role I felt born to play.

If they said anything I didn't like the sound of, I'd say something like: "I'm not seeing you, bye." I could hear them talking at hundred miles an hour, begging me not to hang up.

Some men wouldn't take no for an answer. After one rejection, I saw a card slide through my letterbox. 'Please see me,' it read, 'I'm waiting around the corner.'

If the appointment was at 2pm and they arrived at 1.55, I'd say: "You're early. I'm not seeing you now."

The next time they'd arrive bang on 2pm (sometimes I'd spot a client walking up and down the street, nervously checking his watch), sometimes breathless after having run to make it on time.

Then I'd wait with the door on the chain, deciding whether to open it, delighted by their disbelieving faces. Access into my world had to be on my terms. Besides, logistics were all important, if anyone was early or late it could throw out a delicately balanced schedule on a packed day.

As a result, I ended up with dozens of men obsessed with me. I arrived home one day to find I'd had 16 missed calls from the same number. "Oh hello Natalie," the most recent message said, "I just wanted to hear your voice so I listened to your voicemail recording over and over again."

*

I was at a particular branch of Waitrose, doing a food and booze shop. I'd never leave the house without being made up and in heels and that went for food shopping too.

As I was studying the shelves, a man reached over my shoulder, brushing my skin. He smiled, winked and said: "Sorry Mistress."

Another man started following me around the shop.

"What are you doing?" I demanded. He smiled nervously and scurried away.

This turned out to be a major pick up venue, that's how it seemed to me, men who were into domination or a quick lay.

Back in the day, gay men repressed their urges as best as they could and got married – and in my experience they tend to choose women who looked like men.

My experiences have given me excellent Gaydar and often when men came to see me I could tell immediately that they would soon be asking me for men. In fact, I'd say that nine out of ten men who came to me had fantasies of being with men and, with my help most of them acted them out.

They even let me take pictures of them in compromising positions, sometimes with other men, particularly when they were with Blue; some would try and hide their faces, but they usually ended up in the photos.

One such character was John 'P', who worked for an Investment Company in the City and lived in Chelsea. He wasn't a spring chicken by any means, but had plenty of energy. He was public school educated and had improved the already considerable family fortune through his investments.

I first met JP through Madam C, when he called up to ask for a young black girl.

Our relationship started with normal sex but he quickly revealed he was into domination, which included being chained to a four-poster bed, and showed me into his bedroom, where, inside a wardrobe, was every single kind of chain and whip you can imagine.

And then one day, after not having seen him for years, he rang Black Beauties.

"Natalie, it's John P, do you remember me? I'd love to see you."

"Hi John, of course I remember. What can I do for you?"

"I was hoping you could fit me in this Friday evening for a session."

I checked my diary. "Sure, I can do that, as long as you can wait until 8pm."

"There's one thing though, there's another girl I'd like to be there, someone else I've been seeing."

"Oh yeah?"

"Yeah, she's a supermodel."

I could hear the pride in his voice. I wasn't impressed. How much of a supermodel could she be if she's hooking?

"Fine. I'll come but you have to pay me the same as whatever she's getting."

A brief pause, then: "Alright then."

When I arrived at JP's house the supermodel was already there. She was extremely tall, close to six foot, bad hair extensions

I could immediately tell she wasn't into domination, her demeanour was all wrong – passive and disinterested, with half-hearted whip waving. I tried to get her to whip JP's ass off but she just wasn't into it, so I took over.

I later asked her why, when she was such a famous model and not into domination, she had taken the job. It seemed that work as a model was intermittent, and she

had a life style to maintain, today she's a very successful business woman, there are a few woman I've come across both past and present that are or were famous in my line of work, there's a broadsheet journalist I personally know of that had to let's say 'make ends meet' and have a past they'd like to forget. I worked in the same 'gentlemen's club' as she did many moons ago, the very one run by Connie the ex-priest.

"How much are you getting for this anyway?" I asked.

"£3,000 per session."

Okay, not bad at all!

I now knew then that A) JP was even wealthier than I thought, and B) he was getting me cheap, so I upped his fee from that day forth, which was just as well because he made me do some very weird stuff.

In fact, he was a strange creature in general. He picked up all his meals from a famous local restaurant adjacent to his house most evenings but when I went into his tiny but perfectly-formed designer kitchen (the make was Smallbone and he told me that it had cost him £25,000), for another bottle of champagne and looked in his fridge there was a very sad looking piece of meat, some bones, a potato and a bit of broccoli on a plate.

"What the hell's this?"

He was slightly embarrassed. "It's been there for a few days I'll eat it later. I grew up during rationing and was taught to make use of every scrap of food."

I didn't understand how someone so rich was able to keep leftovers in a fridge for so long.

We started to talk about food and he revealed how he hated semolina.

"There's no way on earth I would ever eat that again. I have a complete horror of the stuff; it makes me want to vomit."

Top tip: Never tell a dominatrix there's something you're terrified of or won't 'ever' do again.

If you can eat what's on that plate, I thought, then you can have semolina.

The next time JP booked me to come to his house, I came prepared - but I have to admit that JP definitely surprised me when he threw open the door to reveal he was dressed in a maid's uniform – with stockings suspenders, a frilly pinafore and, I noticed painted nails. I was dubious as

116

to whether he had painted them himself.

His front door opened right onto Elms Place, on the corner of the eternally busy Fulham Road, but he didn't seem to mind being seen.

Normally, I'm not freaked out by anything but I found JP's get up most disturbing. He was an old man in makeup and heels that turned him into a tottering giant, a perverted, smudged lipstick very unattractive maid

Oddly, considering the lengths to which he'd gone, he wasn't wearing a wig – as he was nearly bald, I thought that should have been near the top of his list.

"Hello Mistress."

Recovering, I helloed back at the freak show and stepped inside. He had changed all the lightbulbs in his house to red in some rooms and green in the bathroom, whatever possessed him! Making the scene even more odd (even though I quite liked the effect and made a note to get some for myself).

"What would you like to drink?" He asked. "And then can I make you something to eat?"

"Champagne."

"Of course. I'm here to do your bidding, madam."

For once I was really thrown. I really wasn't sure how to play this one.

"If there's anything else you'd like, don't hesitate to instruct me."

He then passed me a piece of paper, upon which was a list of how he wanted the evening to go. The game JP wanted to play was to serve me but at the same time he was telling me what to do – that definitely didn't work for me.

If I was going to strip off and go to work for him, I wasn't going to do it his frigging way.

I quickly drank the champagne and stood up.

"You're going to take off the ridiculous clothes and

dress like a slave – what are you, a fucking woman?"

JP stopped smiling and crumbled as though his spine had collapsed.

"Yes Mistress, yes Mistress, yes Mistress," was all he could say.

We went upstairs to the bedroom, which in his wardrobe was every kind of bondage gear one would ever need.

"What would you like me to wear, Mistress?"

"Just get undressed and wash off the makeup."

When he came back out of the bathroom I said: "I've got a surprise for you."

"What's that madam?"

The minute he saw what it was, he knew he shouldn't have mentioned it.

"Please, don't tell me its semolina."

He looked as though a man in a ski mask carrying a bloody axe had just walked into the room.

"Yes it is and you're going to fucking eat it."

"I'd rather be skinned alive!"

He turned white and started to shake.

"Nonsense! Here, eat it or I will punish you like never before."

I couldn't believe that semolina was causing such an extreme reaction. The session would crumble if I gave in, so there was no way I was going to back down, no matter what.

"Dip your tongue in it to start with."

"No! Never!"

I slapped him across the face.

"You're going to be punished slave, if you're not going to eat it."

He was forgetting all about the domination; I could only see sheer, blind terror.

I took a cane out of the wardrobe and started whacking

118

his arse as punishment. This had the effect of bringing him back into the game; he thought we were moving on, but we hadn't. Once he was whimpering in delight I handcuffed him to the bed – arms and legs – so he was spread-eagled on his back.

I fetched the pot of semolina.

"If you don't eat this, I won't untie you and your housekeeper, will find you like this tomorrow."

"Never!"

"Take it!"

I had warmed it but now it had grown cold and was even more hideous to him. Ignoring his horrified pleas, I pressed the spoon between his lips, which remained pressed shut tight, so I clamped his nose with my other hand and waited.

JP trembled and shook as he tried to hold his breath, turning purple, when he finally had to give in and I shoved the spoon into his mouth, clamped his nose again so he had to swallow to breathe.

"Swallow it slave!"

He shook his head. I spat over his face. He squirmed and jerked, trying to resist.

"Swallow it slave!"

He swallowed.

"Aaaaargh!" He screamed. "I'm going to be sick."

"No you're not," I told him. "You're going to eat every last drop."

"No, I'll do anything now, anything but that, please!"

This was one of those moments where I could really have taken advantage and exploited JP's terror of semolina for my own financial gain – but it never occurred to me to do so. I didn't want to exploit my clients – I loved my job. I only wanted to give them a domination experience they would never forget.

I clipped on some nipple clamps, the nasty ones with metal teeth and a merciless winding mechanism that drove them into the skin. I turned until he screamed, and the next spoon went in.

"No complaints or I'll make them tighter!"

He swallowed, moaning and sobbing. I tightened the clips again and he screamed, tears streaking his cheeks as the next cold spoonful went in.

Finally, after the last mouthful, I leaned in close and looked JP in the eye.

"Don't ever tell me what you don't like," I said.

He just lay there, gasping on the bed.

The session was over. I un-cuffed him, got changed and left without another word.

*

JP called a few days later to make another booking. He knew, like all the others, that there was no dominatrix in the world who was more serious, more committed and more determined than me. I was the real deal.

We saw each other for years afterwards but I never did find out why he was so horrified of semolina. He had a lot of guilt; he said he was a bad father for leaving his wife to raise their two sons, one of whom was autistic, on her own.

The more I got to know JP, the more perverted he became. He was into men, domination, dressing up, pissing in his mouth, there was no boundary he was too scared to cross.

After I'd been seeing JP for a couple of years he asked:

"Can you get me younger girls?"

"How young?"

"As young as you can get."

120

I'd send him girls that looked really young but were in their twenties.

"Lie about your age," I told them. "Tell him you're 18."

He wasn't the only client who ever expressed an interest in underage girls but thankfully I never got the impression he pursued it and he seemed satisfied with the girls I sent him.

I would really have left him chained up for the maid to find him that day. As it turned out, he allegedly kept another hooker he'd been seeing imprisoned, locked up in the self-contained flat in the basement part of his house. She escaped and sold her story to a Sunday newspaper. JP once told me, in a most menacing tone, that if anyone ever tried to write a story about him again, they'd be in "big trouble." WOOPS!

## Seventeen

# CRAZY LOVE

Imagine if you will, an exclusive dinner party in the county among exceedingly wealthy middle-aged bankers and lawyers.

The host John and his wife are into domination. They've arranged to see me the next day and are looking forward to it immensely.

The phone rings. It's me, calling to confirm our rendezvous at Blakes Hotel. Not wanting to interrupt the party, John lets the machine get it. They always leave it at full volume, so they can hear it wherever they are in the house.

"Hi John, it's Natalie."

Now picture the looks on both John's and his wife's faces. Domination is their secret. They do not want their ultra-conservative friends to find out. Both of them believe that their lives would be over if it was discovered.

"I'm looking forward to meeting you both tomorrow at Blakes-"

John and his wife had by now leapt up from the table and were engaging each other in an inelegant trying-not-to-look-too-desperate sprint for the phone.

"So don't forget your paddle, will you? Or to br-"

John's hand slapped down the mute button.

"-ing the coke."

The next day, it was me who got the telling-off. I tried not to laugh as I asked John how he explained my message to his guests.

"They asked us about the paddle and I had to make something up about a rowing club."

I tried to sound contrite through my giggles and then imagined the look on his guests' faces. It hadn't dawned on me that leaving a message could get John into trouble.

"Sorry John, I really fucked up!"

"It's okay, I should've picked up the phone."

*

I'd been seeing John for two years when he told me he wanted to bring his wife. I wasn't surprised that she knew about John's love of domination. I'd sent him home with some severe bruises, welts and bleeding nipples dozens of times.

I once asked him: "What will your wife say when she sees you with those marks?"

He shrugged. "If she sees them, she sees them."

Sometimes my clients would confess their secrets to their wives. This would lead to one of three reactions.

They could:

1.  Accept their husband's love of domination for what it was.
2.  Get into it as well.
3.  Sue for divorce.

Numbers 1 and 3 were the most popular choices. It was unusual for a wife to want to join in but John assured me she was really into the whole thing, so I agreed.

Blakes hotel was discreet as always and gave us a basement room with its own street entrance, so we didn't have to come in the front.

I met John first in the bar. Then I went ahead into the basement room while John's wife joined him at the bar. She then telephoned me in the room to check all was ready and they came down to and join me. John later told me that his wife had said she was surprised to hear my accent, which she thought was quite educated, in other words not common. How was she expecting me to sound?

Unfortunately I didn't find his wife attractive at all. She was far too boney for my taste with tits the size of golf balls. She had with her a case containing all her own paraphernalia.

We retired to the room and his wife changed into a patent leather dress, dog collar and heels.

I started to feel awkward. John was my slave and I wanted to do my thing with him but now his wife was involved and he was trying to show her off to me as his! slave. Throughout the evening I was John's Mistress and in control of him. This couldn't have felt good for her; she was right at the bottom of the food chain but she seemed to be into the whole thing – if she was acting, she was good.

At some point into the evening John's wife and I pleasured each other, while John watched and masturbated, his wife and I both took control of John, taking turns in dishing out his punishment, it was clear that they both indulged in S&M with each other regularly, usually on a Saturday night, I just wasn't interested in her. She was skeletal and I prefer my women to be voluptuous. I nevertheless decided to do what she asked, as they were paying.

This situation felt strange to me – despite the fact John was enjoying himself immensely, I felt as though his wife was playing along. Surely she couldn't be happy about my presence, let alone what I was doing to her husband? Perhaps she thought that a black hooker wasn't a threat to her – and that the domination just a little kink in her otherwise perfect husband. But John and I had been seeing one another for two years by this time – did she know it had been that long?

I was convinced that there was no way any woman who still had feelings for her husband was going to be happy with him seeing another woman like this, and – she was in fact doing all this for her husband.

Now that was a crazy kind of love.

# Eighteen

# MONTE CARLO

I strode through a sunlit Nice Airport in killer heels, short summer dress, Versace overnight bag, nine beautiful girls in my wake, heading for the limousine for the final leg of our journey to the Hotel Metropole in Monte Carlo. I could feel the heads turning.

We pulled up at the Metropole, which overlooks the cream-coloured stone buildings of Casino Square, home to the belle époque Disney castle that is the Monte Carlo Casino, used by Ian Fleming in his first Bond novel, Casino Royale.

Impossibly expensive sports cars glided through wide and spotlessly clean streets; as we drew up to the 5-star hotel, I felt the rollercoaster rush of excitement in anticipation of the debauched 5-star adventure that lay ahead – especially the huge financial reward.

We were there for the client my girls and I had christened 'Mr. Twist', one of Britain's wealthiest men – a billionaire, and has been made a Knight. All Mr. Twist's girls had to be black, slim (size 10-12), in suspenders and high-heels. So I brought Sonya, a tall, sharp-witted woman who worked for a large media agency, (now a PA in the city) and fucked like a demon; almond-eyed Peggy from Zambia, who couldn't read or write in English but could make a man come fifty different ways and Carol, angular and as cold as ice, whose favourite way to get laid was to part her legs and command 'Fuck me,' and who delighted in dealing with the cruellest, most demanding clients (Mr. Twist was the most demanding of all). Then there was super-fit Catherine who could lift her own bodyweight and was very good at domination – not squeamish about causing pain. Then there was also Claire, Jackie, Yvonne, Alex (an illegal immigrant from Nigeria who travelled on visitors' passport in the name of Tracy) and Patricia.

We were all tall, wearing killer heels and sections of our smooth skin were showing in all the right places. We were fearless, deadly and ready to work like no other ladies could.

We checked in under the eyes of a snooty young receptionist who could not believe that we had reservations in this 5-Star institution. She knew we were hookers and did not like that fact we had reservations – hookers are not supposed to book rooms.

I smiled my thank you a little too sweetly once the receptionist finally handed us our swipe keys.

"I'm starved," Peggy – who was always hungry - said, "Let's get some lunch."

"Our set lunch is 2,000 Francs madam," the receptionist answered snobbily.

"No problem," I replied brightly, "We'll need six of those – and some champagne."

But to our surprise and disgust, no waiter would serve us in the restaurant. It was as if we did not exist.

The problem? Our colour. The Metropole was snobby in all senses, class, wealth and race.

"Fuck this girls," I said. "We can order service from our rooms."

A team of handsome young men in smart uniforms

delivered our lunches. Mr. Twist had told us to sign off everything to him, so we did just that.

Then I had an idea. As I handed the young man the signed bill I said, "I've added a little something extra for all your trouble."

"There's really no-"

Shocked by the amount, he'd stopped talking mid-sentence.

I'd tipped them £100 each. After that, the waiters, concierge, maids and managers couldn't scramble to our assistance fast enough, no matter where we were and what we needed, and so we kept signing £100 tips, which proves if you've enough of it, money conquers all, even racism.

All of us had separate rooms. The bed was the most comfortable I ever had the pleasure of sleeping in; the shower had jets coming at you from every conceivable angle, so one emerged massaged and, depending which way you turned, thoroughly stimulated.

I simply had to play the roulette wheel at 'Casino Royale', so visited the gambler's paradise where I learned that the citizens of Monaco are forbidden to enter – the doormen wouldn't let me in without seeing my passport.

I was in full Bond-girl-attire, figure hugging dress and few thousand in chips. After a pleasurable hour or so, I returned to my hotel room, where Peggy and Carol joined me. To pass the time, we ordered caviar and champagne.

There was a knock at the door.

"That was quick," Peggy said. But instead of a handsome young bellhop (the Metropole seemed to choose its staff straight from a catalogue of models), a smartly dressed young man in an Armani suit entered the room: "Hello, you must be Natalie. I've got a delivery for Mr. Twist, may I use your bathroom?"

"Er…Sure."

He emerged a few minutes later and handed me a king-sized lipstick container.

"What's this?"

"The coke."

Mr. Twist had paid £1,500 to have his own trusted supplier get it to Monaco for him.

"Ah. Why is it in a lipstick container?"

He smiled. "I had to get it through the airport somehow, let's just say it was well hidden"

"What? Oh crap, yeah I see," I said dropping it to the bed.

"I cleaned it."

"Well, I'm not keeping it in my room."

Armed with the coke, wearing black heels and suspenders under our dresses, we made our way to Mr. Twist's room.

Our mood was electric – we knew if we did what was expected of us, then we would be leaving with a huge amount of cash.

The problem was, getting that money from him wasn't easy.

Mr. Twist, who was beyond middle age, of average height and build and mostly bald, seemed like a genial middle-aged man in public. But I never got to see that side of him.

I only ever got to see one part of his personality.

He was fierce, furious and wanted something extraordinary from us.

Mr. Twist didn't want sex.

Not exactly.

We entered a huge suite. It was surrounded by buckets of champagne.

On the bed was a large leather suitcase, with lock and clasps.

I couldn't help but eye it hungrily.

Mr. Twist was kneeling on the bed, naked with his cock pointing in our direction. It was of average length and girth, but looked so hard it was fit to burst.

"About fucking time," he growled, as if struggling to contain his rage. "Get over here and give me a fucking line."

I got to work with the coke while the girls stripped to suspenders and high heels.

Mr. Twist eyed them, a glazed desperation in his eyes.

Carol was Mr. Twist's golden girl. She had the perfect figure but was cold as ice and gave as good as she got – better usually – if a man tried to mistreat her, physically or verbally.

She walked to the end of the bed, her heels forcing her bottom up into a pair of near-perfect ovals; her skin shone in the golden lamplight as she bent over towards the kneeling billionaire.

"DO IT!" he screamed suddenly, making me jump, spilling some of the coke.

Carol bent forward and reached with both hands for his cock, clasping it firmly; then in a movement that would make any normal man scream, she squeezed, twisted and, at the same time, pulled his member heavenwards, stretching the already rigid cock towards the ornately decorated ceiling. She released it and repeated, and again, and again, finding a rhythm in this bizarre manoeuvre.

"That's it," he sighed. Carol twisted and pulled, Mr. Twist's face grew redder and redder (but not as red as his cock) as he moaned and then shouted until –

"ENOUGH!"

At this, he threw open the large black suitcase. It was full to the brim with cash in a variety of currencies. Carol leapt, fast as lightning. The idea was to take out as much cash as possible before he snapped the heavy case shut –

and to avoid getting caught in its jaws. Carol snatched two big handfuls and leapt back as Mr. Twist roared "AAAARGH!" and practically dived on the suitcase, slamming it closed.

"You next, bitch!" he said, beckoning Sonia over.

"You don't tell me what to fucking do you little fucking stuck-up prick," Sonia answered.

'Nicely said,' I thought.

This was all part of the game, to give as good as you got. Sonia walked over, bent towards him, grabbed his balls with one hand and slapped his red face with the other, then grabbed hold of his cock with both and started twisting upwards.

"NO! THAT'S NO FUCKING GOOD!" Mr. Twist screamed at the top of his voice. I hoped the walls were soundproofed. "GIVE ME ANOTHER FUCKING LINE AND THEN THIS TIME FUCKING TWIST IT HARDER! I WANT YOU TO- AAARGH!"

For a terrible moment I thought Sonia had pulled so hard, she'd yanked Mr. Twist's cock off, but no, he was enjoying himself once more.

I still have absolutely no idea why this turned him on so. We weren't paid to analyse; we were there to twist as much money out of him as we could.

Soon, we were all drenched in sweat; empty champagne bottles lay strewn across the floor; we drank quickly because we were so hot from all the twisting, plus we weren't allowed to relax, not for a hot minute. Mr Twist was on his back and I was twisting, twisting, twisting – my arms ached so much I could barely keep the movement going – but there was still so much money in that suitcase.

"ENOUGH!"

He held the suitcase open and in I dived, emerging with two large fistfuls of dollars.

We had to stay straight-backed the whole time, no slouching or any slacking was allowed otherwise he'd shout abuse: "You fucking lazy black bitch, straighten up you lazy cow."

The reason I brought so many girls was so I could rotate them in shifts (as this was tiring work) and every so often Mr. Twist would shout: "You can fuck off! Natalie, get me another one of your black bitches!"

Mr. Twist would never come, just always on the edge, interrupting any potentially climatic moments with a scream and then another "AAARGH!" as he snapped the suitcase shut.

And on it went. Twist, Scream, Plunge, Scream, Slam, Twist, Scream, Plunge, Scream, Slam, Twist, Scream, Plunge, Scream, Slam.

In the small hours, Mr. Twist was joined by a couple of trusted friends who'd spent the evening gambling. He told Carol and Claire to go fuck these men, which they promptly did, Carol doing coke as one of the men did her from behind, while Claire snorted a line off the other man's erect cock, and while Claire twisted away, while I sat back with a glass of bubbly and watched this impossible-to-imagine scene unfold in this 5-star setting. I don't think this room had ever seen so much action.

As we staggered back to our rooms after the session was over, we debated what to do with the cocaine.

"I'll stash it," Peggy volunteered. She took the lipstick and went to her room.

The next day, when it was time for Mr. Twist's next session and I went to see if the girls were ready. Peggy had a 'Do Not Disturb' sign on the door and wouldn't answer.

I should have known. Peggy was too much of a coke fiend to resist. I didn't think she would have been so stupid as to snort the whole lot, let alone have the energy after our

132

marathon session with Mr. Twist. We could hardly smash down the door and we didn't want to call room service to open it, for fear of what they might find inside. In the end, we 'tipped' a friendly bellhop to let us in. Peggy was flat out on the bed, unable to speak, surrounded by rolled up notes, the lipstick (empty) and all the bottles from the minibar. I heaved her into a sitting position.

"Peggy you stupid fucking cow!"

I waved my hand in front of her face.

"Peggy? Are you in there, girl?"

I slapped her. She woke up at last, huge pupils that struggled to focus; she mumbled incomprehensibly.

I had to think quickly, we needed more Charlie or the booking was VERY FUCKING over and a lot of MONEY lost!

You know what's the best thing about money? Answer - having access to any amount you need to solve a problem, so a phone call was made, someone hopped on a plane, and bang in time for our next session with our BILLIONAIRE!

The following evening, arms throbbing, barely able to hold our overnight bags and some somehow half-carrying Peggy (who'd somehow already managed to blow a good amount of her fee on Christian Dior outfits) between us, we drove back to Nice airport - with a bit more baggage than we came with: over a hundred grand in crumpled notes of all denominations, some of which smelt like a cocaine den.

Back in the day when I had moved to Montague Square, I had a visitor, who wanted to have the life twisted out of his penis, that very man was the very man I'd just left back in Monaco, I didn't remind him of that encounter, all I know is he didn't pay me anywhere near what I'd just pocketed, glad to see he was still doing the rounds and considerably richer!

# Nineteen

# BEST OF FIVE

"Hi Natalie, come on in."

Timothy was slim, about 5'9", had dark, slightly receding hair and seemed to have a penchant for beige or cream linen suits, as that's all he ever wore every time I saw him. He lived in South Kensington. In fact about 2/3 Years ago having had no contact with Timothy for decades, on my way to Marks & Spencer on Kensington High St, there he was, and I kid you not he was in his obligatory linen suit! he was clearly eyeing me up, I didn't believe he remembered me, but I do think he was on the prowl for a challenger, just an instinctive feeling I got, having never talked about work and I doubted he had a job, just a trust fund. He'd definitely been a spoiled child.

I entered his flat and we made our way straight to the spacious lounge. In the middle of the room, on the floor, was a mattress. We got changed. We both wore shorts and nothing else. There was very little in the way of formality with Timothy, he never offered a glass of wine and I would never have accepted. I needed a clear head if I was going to emerge victorious.

My body was still aching from the last time I'd seen Timothy, four days earlier.

Most of my girls refused to see him - Timothy only

wanted to see me if possible, I was the only one who took his peccadillo very seriously – and the only one he'd been unable to defeat.

Timothy's heart's desire was to wrestle. Five rounds, £100 per round for me, each round ending only when one of us cried "Surrender!"

We squared up to one another. Round one!

Today, I thought to myself, I'm not going to mess around. Go in hard and fast, win, take my money and go. I still hadn't quite recovered from our last encounter and still ached with a few fading bruises as a reminder and wanted to get the whole thing over with as fast as possible.

By round five we were sweating and exhausted, panting for breath. I'd got the better of Timothy and had him in a headlock. I'd won the first four and was desperate to get this over as soon as possible – but my energy was depleting fast, while Timothy, although weaker than me, still had more energy, he was really heated today.

But, as far as I was concerned, this was the fifth and final round and I was determined to end it.

"Surrender!"

"No!"

"Surrender, say it! or I won't let go! No!"

"Fucking surrender. Did you really think you were stronger than me? Say it or I'll squeeze harder."

He wriggled and kicked like a madman.

"Timothy, I'm not going to let go!"

"I surrender!" He finally caved but added, spitting the words out, pointing his finger at me: "You're a cheat. A lousy, stinking cheat!"

"Whatever. You surrendered five times, fair and square."

"I want another five rounds."

"Are you paying for that?"

"Yes."

I thought about it. I was exhausted, sore and aching, but I couldn't bring myself to leave here without £1,000.

"Okay then tough guy, let's go!"

I won the first two but when we got to round three, he threw me onto the mattress and sat on me, straddling my arms, pinning me down.

I couldn't move.

"Surrender!"

"No!"

"Surrender!"

I was so angry that he'd got me into this position. There was no way I could bear to let him win, the little shit, I was furious, I somehow found a reserve of strength in my shoulders, wiggled and pushed and – threw him off! I shoved him to one side and, as he toppled, I rolled over on top of him – now our positions were reversed as I moved up to his chest and sat on him, pushing down with all my weight, suffocating him with my breasts.

"Mmmnmmpff!"

"What? I can't hear you!"

"Mmmmmpfferer!"

"What?"

I sat back.

"I surrender!" he squealed.

We got up. Now it was round four. I was sweating, exhausted.

"I need a glass of water."

"No!" Timothy yelled back. "No fucking water, it's round four now."

I was pissed off. Two rounds still to go.

We both stood on the edge of the mattress, sweating, panting, staring each other out – now it was deadly serious.

Timothy dived forward and grabbed my arms; we

grappled, panting. He had the better of me. I was out of energy, he was going to win, but still I found a tiny reserve and I shoved him back before charging him with a roar – I took him so much by surprise that he was unable to resist and with him now half falling, half running backwards, we charged right to the other end of the room and crashed straight through his beautiful antique cherry wood desk, clearly now in need of restoration, I sat up and Timothy, on the floor but still not done, enraged, looked like he was ready to kill. 'Oh God,' I thought, 'He's going to kill me!' but at that moment a crystal-ball-sized paperweight rolled off and landed straight on his head.

There was no round five.

As I limped down the road, £1,000 in my handbag, leaving poor old Timothy nursing one hell of a lump, I thought to myself that there must be easier ways to earn a living.

# Twenty

# SAD NEWS

I once left Fidenzes with two girlfriends and started to drive my VW Golf the back to my place in Maida Vale when I was pulled over by two male cops in an unmarked car in a side street off Bond Street. They'd seen me leaving the club and thought I was going to be over the limit. I hadn't drunk much but I was definitely pushing it, so I tried sweet-talking them.

They'd been quite friendly and we were having a laugh with them about something or other when I said: "You've been out here all night having a boring time, why don't you forget about this and come back to mine for a drink and a bit of a party?"

They looked at one another.

"Come on," I said, standing back so they could see the other two girls I was with. They were good looking women – one black, the other blonde.

"Alright then," the older one said. "You drive and we'll follow. Try not to kill anyone, okay?"

So, with their permission, I drove, very carefully back home – it was only then that I remembered little Klaus had cut his foot on some broken glass the night before and there was a huge wet bloodstain on my beige carpet in the lounge, with a trail of blood all the way to the bathroom.

But they said nothing as we all went in and started having a few drinks. They were in their late twenties, slim and strong, one had an Irish accent, the other English and I quite liked the look of him.

During our very late night conversation, it was well after 4 in the morning, and both cops were now drinking with us

I said, "Have you ever stitched anyone up?"

"Of course," the Irish one said. "I've planted weed on someone who gave me too much grief in past."

The other officer had the decency to at least look uncomfortable.

They were with us for about couple of hours and when they finally got up to leave, the English officer left his number with me. "Perhaps we can go out sometime," he suggested.

I actually dialled his number the next morning but hung up just before it started to ring. It probably wasn't such a good idea...

*

I would usually go beyond what clients thought they could take – there's a fine line between ecstasy and agony. If you can't find it, then you're not doing the job right.

Sometimes, however, even I could push this a little too far. Once I couldn't find the thin needle I used to put through heads of some of my clients' cocks.

This was a surprisingly popular request but certainly wasn't for the faint of heart. I had no problem doing this, except on this occasion, as I rummaged through the bathroom I was unable to find the thin needle. So I shrugged and took a thicker one.

"Here I am! Are you ready?"

The client in question in this case was Christopher the art dealer with the grotty flat. He was standing and his penis slightly aroused, dangling between his legs.

"Yes Mistress, yes."

I sat on a chair in front of him and put a bit of coke over the end of his cock to numb it a bit.

Then, I lined up the needle, pressed the point against the purple skin and, with my lips pressed together in concentration, started to force it through. The secret was to maintain a steady hand, to not stop and push it through at a consistent pace. As usual, it slid through the flesh as though it were lamb's liver.

"AAAAAAAAAAAARGH!"

"Hold still, stop screaming!"

It became a little bit trickier once halfway through, but I maintained speed and pressure, my concentration total - I ignored the shrieking, I only had ears for the safe word.

"Mistresssss!!!"

No safe word, so I continued, until the point broke the skin on the other side. I can't imagine what the pain must have been like – especially while it was still in the flesh. Christopher's eyes were bulging and his whole body shook as if in shock, but he was the happiest man alive.

I thought I'd got away with it – Christopher Hewitt hadn't noticed the difference in the needle's diameter but after I withdrew it, his penis wouldn't stop bleeding. There was a veritable fountain of blood, in fact, so much so that I was ready to call an ambulance, but Christopher begged for his secrecy, so we compressed and held some ice against it and crossed our fingers until the bleeding finally stopped.

My relationship with Christopher was not a healthy one. He was addicted to me and I was addicted to his money. The man bought me a mink coat and then a gold-coloured BMW for God's sake, how could I stop seeing him?

He became a regular after that first time – and he had been the first client of mine to demand the most severe and bizarre sexual acts from me. It was clear then that I had the natural propensity for domination (although I didn't know that such a thing existed right at the beginning – Chris was just another weird client).

It was soon clear I hadn't even scratched the surface in terms of his desire to be dominated. With a few days the needles had appeared – these were for his nipples at first.

He was delighted that I was as fearless as he was (he worshipped me) and was up for anything – as long as he wanted pain, then by whatever means he wanted to feel it, I had no problem with doing it to him.

So the first time he asked me to put a needle through the head of his penis, I only asked him if he was sure the once. I also put toothpaste and tabasco down his urethra.

Christopher drank my urine and worse, he asked for the grossest things I've ever witnessed: what had happened in his life to make him want to do this sort of thing.

I was the only one who would do whatever Christopher wanted and as a result he became addicted to me. Normally, if a client bored me or started to creep me out, I'd up my prices so much that they'd stop calling. Money meant nothing to Christopher, however and he paid so much that I couldn't bring myself to stop seeing him.

Sometimes he'd make me stay for hours beyond the time we agreed and ran out of cash with which to pay me, so he'd write a cheque.

"Don't cash it," he'd say. "Meet me outside Mappin and Webb Knightsbridge tomorrow afternoon and I'll pay you in cash and you can give me back the cheque."

Sure enough, that's what we did. Mappin and Webb, a luxury jewellers, used to have a shop just around the corner from his gallery, and our meeting there became a frequent occurrence. Chris always wore corduroy; the type that the upper classes seem to love, mustard yellow, reds and soft pink.

By the time Christopher started freebasing cocaine during our sessions I'd had enough of him. The sessions were exhausting and I needed longer breaks because he was so demanding - it felt as though he was taking over my life. He didn't want it to end; he wanted and assumed it would carry on like this forever.

Eventually, after a long session when he begged me to stay longer I decided to ask for something really crazy: "If I'm going to stay I want £100 per minute."

He agreed without a moment's hesitation and he handed over an additional £6,000 in cash at Mappin and Webb the next day.

Christopher was a stubborn man. He once ran out of coke when I was with him and asked me if I knew a place where he could score some more.

"I can take you to a dealer, if you like."

"OK," he said before adding: "Is this dealer the sort of guy who could get me a man?"

This was interesting, he hadn't asked for a man before. It turned out that he didn't want a man sexually, not exactly. Christopher wanted a man to beat him up; it was all part of the domination.

"Well, this dealer's good, but I don't know if he's that good."

So I went to Ladbroke Grove with my friend Shel to see this guy. I explained Chris's request and the dealer was actually able to help me, with a young black man – so Shel and me brought him back to Chris's flat. As we were sitting there, sorting out the coke, out of the fucking blue the man pulled out a flick knife.

"Give me your money."

Shel wasn't having it. "Fuck off, there's three of us and one of you."

I just wanted to get out of this alive and was happy to hand over whatever we had – although this guy hadn't seen my bag, which – full of cash - was hidden under the table.

Chris was on Shel's side, however.

"I'm not going to give you any money," he said firmly.

Our roles had suddenly been reversed: I was Miss Submissive and he was the Master now.

"Chris," I said, "Just give him the fucking money."

"You think this is some kind of game?" the guy said, waving the knife.

I kept a gold chain with small custom-made coke spoon on the end of it for snorting (something I'd copied from Cool Black) and he ripped that from my neck. He also took my Gucci watch and black onyx and gold Dupont lighter, then Chris's watch and his bank-cards, which were on the kitchen table.

Chris was still defiant. Shel picked up a brass lampshade, ready to try and brain our robber.

"Shut the fuck up and put that down," I hissed, "I don't want this to escalate. None of this is worth dying for, it's all replaceable."

This seemed to calm things down and our hold-up guy was able to leave in peace – without spotting my bag.

I was still with Rudi at this time and told him what happened. We went back to Ladbroke Grove and waited in the car outside where I'd scored the drugs, a dingy basement room, until I saw the guy.

"That's him."

"Sure?"

"He's wearing my necklace and using my gold Dupont lighter."

Rudi went off and a few minutes later he emerged with

the robber, who had a bloody nose, in an arm lock. I nodded.

This was a nerve-wracking moment as some other guys came out to see what all the excitement was about. Rudi told them to back off, that he had a weapon, so they just watched as Rudi took back the gold chain, lighter and all the drugs he had in his pockets.

This experience turned me somewhat paranoid afterwards; my sixth sense, which I'd thought to be good, had failed to warn me about this robber. One moment, he seemed to be really nice and the next I had a knife at my throat – he literally switched personalities from one moment to the next.

*

Immediately after the robbery, Chris was ready to carry on with the party.

"What about what just happened?" I asked. "Aren't you going to call the police?"

"Are you mad? We have coke. You still need to make money. Let's carry on."

And so we did, from one extreme to the next, after I'd downed copious amounts of brandy.

So, true to his stubborn form, Chris wouldn't stop booking me despite my massive price hikes, and despite Chris's extreme demands, I couldn't stop going for the love of his money.

But it was draining – our sessions, which lasted up to ten hours, taxed me both mentally and physically. A good dominatrix has to be able to customise her routine to each client.

Among his special requests was for me to bring a pre filled bottle of my urine, which he would decant like wine and drink during our session.

After I'd arrived he'd ask: "Please Mistress, which role would you like me to play today?"

"Schoolboy. And because you haven't done your homework I'm going to give you twelve of the best!"

The cane was his and had seen better days but it was still effective.

"Stick your pale fucking arse in the air."

Other clients wanted me to start off gently but not Chris. He wanted a harsh beating from beginning to end. He wasn't happy - and neither was I - until his welts were bleeding.

His best 'reward' would be for me to clamp his head between my strong thighs and squeeze as hard as I could.

The hardest thing that he ever asked me to do was to defecate into his open mouth; it required my full concentration and even I found this act extremely unnatural.

He'd always beg me for more after it was time for me to go. I'd try to leave and he'd plead: "Please mistress, just another hour, please," and sometimes I'd stay once he'd offered me enough money to make it worth my while, but I always needed days to recover after these marathon sessions.

One night I'd planned a night out with some girlfriends and Chris pleaded for me to stay with him a bit longer, offering more money.

"Please, just one more hour, please Mistress."

I'd come to dread the end of our sessions. His begging was really starting to get on my fucking nerves; it had become a real mission for me to just get away.

This time I just looked him in the eye. "No Chris, I have to go now."

He looked absolutely heartbroken.

The next day he wasn't at Mappin and Webb. This was the first time he'd ever failed to turn up so I decided to go around to his flat. I pressed the buzzer and there was no answer, the curtains were drawn and even though it was daylight I could see through a crack in the curtain that the lights were on inside. But he was always a strange one, I thought, so left him to it.

The next day, after still not having heard from him about exchanging his cheque for cash, I went around again. Heather, a friend from Bradford was with me. She was a blonde white hooker who worked for one of Rudi's friends (despite all this, she ended up marrying a policeman).

The lights were still on. Something was wrong. I felt compelled to call the police. I thought about it for a while because I was going to have to explain how and why I knew him and why I was worried.

An officer arrived a few minutes later and eventually broke down the door. He went in while Heather and I waited outside the door.

He came out looking white as a sheet.

"Is he alright?"

"No, he's dead."

Although the worst is always in the back of your mind in these situations, you never think it's actually going to be the case. I was dizzy with shock.

I had been the last person to see Chris alive. He had spent the rest of the night drinking and taking drugs and then choked on his own vomit.

Had I stayed then maybe he'd still be alive today. I'll just never know. Sometimes, even now, I suffer moments of great sadness over poor Christopher. He was so alone, I was all he had to bring him relief from the pain he felt in his life.

At that moment though, I was given a second shock.

146

"You'll have to come down to the station and give a statement."

"What for?"

I'd explained to the policeman how I knew Chris.

"To explain his injuries. At the moment cause of death is unexplained; there'll have to be a coroner's inquest as well and as you were the last person to see him alive you'll need to appear as a witness."

So I went to the police station and sat down with a sergeant and constable. I was going to explain Christopher's injuries to rule out foul play.

"So what was your relationship to the deceased?"

"He paid me for um… certain services."

"Can you be more specific?"

"Well, he liked to be whipped."

"What do you mean he liked to be whipped?"

"I mean that he liked me to whip him with um… A whip."

God, they weren't making this easy.

"And he paid you for this, did he?"

"Yes."

"What else did he like?"

"Well, he liked it when I squeezed his head between my thighs."

The sergeant, who was trying to remain serious, found himself battling to control a smile that was trying very hard to turn into a grin.

"And er… Hmm," he continued. "What else did you do together?"

"I'd spank his bottom with a cane."

"He, hehehe, his bottom."

"Yes, his bottom." I'd started to smile now as well. "And I would put needles through his nipples."

The constable looked mortified. The sergeant's jaw fell

147

open, then he started to giggle, as did I.

"Anything else?"

"Well, yes as a matter of fact. Through his cock and balls too."

The sergeant winced through hissing laughter while the constable turned bright red. He turned round and opened the door to the interview room. "Charlie!" he yelled, "You've got to hear this!"

A plainclothes officer came in. The sergeant turned back to me. "Tell him what you just told me."

So I did.

"Jesus Christ," the plain clothes officer said. "And he paid for this did he?"

I nodded.

"Anything else we should know about?" the sergeant asked.

"Well, maybe."

"Go on."

"Well, he used to drink my urine."

"Get away!"

"And, well, he used to, I used to… That is…"

"Yes?"

"I'd pooh in his mouth."

"What!?!"

All three of them looked appalled, incredulous; grins gone to be replaced by looks of disgust, mouths open.

"I've fucking heard it all now," the plain clothes officer said.

"Thank you Natalie," the sergeant said once we were done, "You've certainly livened up what had been a very dull day."

And my ordeal wasn't over yet. To start with, his family came out of the woodwork and wouldn't let me cash Christopher's cheque and then they tried to claw back the things he'd given me, including the BMW. I hired some lawyers but they were useless and advised me to pay them the money and keep the car, which I did. As far as I was concerned his family were bunch of vultures. They showed no love for him in life and in death only wanted to claw whatever money they could back into their own pockets. I'd liked Chris, despite his weird demands, and he'd always been honest and straight with me. It was such a shame his family were so unpleasant.

Then came the inquest.

I dressed smartly and came to the court where I had to sit in a large room full of people, including lawyers, the coroner, stenographers and various clerks, not to mention members of Chris's family, who already hated me.

I had to go through, step by step, how I met and came to work for Chris, speaking clearly into a microphone. I amassed what mental armour I could and said everything as matter-of-factly as possible. The coroner was being as thorough as possible to make sure there was nothing else that could explain his death apart from drugs and alcohol, which I understood, but then he asked about all the strange objects, such as dildos etc.

Chris' secret life was now all out into the open for his family to hear

I was mortified.

"Miss Rowe, I don't understand. Would you be so good as to be both clear and precise?"

Oh good grief. Right then.

This went on for what seemed eternity

The coroner looked at me for a long moment. "Thank you Miss Rowe, that will be all. You can leave now."

It was all I could do not to run but I walked out slowly, head held high and then got the hell home as fast as humanly possible.

## Twenty One

# REUNITED

Major Ronald Ferguson, father of Sarah Ferguson (then still the Duchess of York) – also a former Guards' officer in Her Majesty's Household Cavalry and Prince Charles's polo manager – was caught by the News of the World coming out of a massage parlour. The galloping Major admitted he'd been a member of the exclusive Wigmore ("health") Club based in London's West End, where white-uniformed "attendants" took care of their clients' every need once they'd paid their 'entrance fee'.

The guy running it was a client of mine and he sent me one or two of his clients after this scandal broke because he wanted to keep a slightly lower profile. He'd come to me to be dominated but said he already had another mistress. "Every now and then, she'll call you after I've left and will ask you questions about me, like was I good slave, did I behave myself and so on."

"No problem," I said, "I'll be happy to."

When the call came, however, I quickly realised that it was him putting on a woman's voice. I played along as if I didn't know and the next time he asked me all about it. He truly believed he was fooling me.

He ended up calling so regularly that I thought he was going a bit too far. He was getting a free booking out of me and so I wouldn't always talk to "her". I'd say something like "I'm busy, I can't be talking to you all the time," but I still took a call every now and again for the fun of it.

One of the men he sent was Simon (the Mini driver from Chapter Seven) and I met him at the Gore Hotel in Queensgate. His full name was Simon Cadell and he had become famous across the UK after starring in Hi-de-Hi! - the holiday-camp sit-com as public school posh-boy twit Jeffrey Fairbrother, the object of his assistant Gladys Pugh's affections.

It was about a decade earlier that we met on Park Lane, when I was still an underage teenager and he'd been filming Enemy at the Gate. Understandably, a lot of water had gone under the bridge, and he didn't remember me. I was tempted to say, "Do you remember you used to drive a Mini around Mayfair?" but decided not to bring it up in the end.

He was just as friendly as before but I also found that he'd become a little lecherous and seedy. He was less tender and not as shy and quiet – and he seemed to think he was king of the castle, which was perhaps not entirely unjustified as he'd just won an Olivier Award playing a leading role in Travels With My Aunt, a play based on the novel by Graham Greene.

He even invited me to see him perform. I went with Peggy – we were the only two black people in the audience and Peggy - who was coked off her head as usual - fell asleep. I sat through the whole thing admittedly bored off my tits, trying to look as interested as possible out of politeness.

I saw Simon about once a month over several years. I also introduced him to other girls. He always booked the rooms under his real name, which surprised me. He was completely hedonistic and loved amyl nitrate and cocaine, chain-smoked cigarettes and cigars and became more and more adventurous, pushing the boundaries of deviancy - he liked to lick my bum which was fine, but then wanted to kiss me – that was never going to happen, so at that point I started sending other girls in my place.

I cried the day in 1996 when I discovered that Simon had died aged just 45 from non-Hodgkins lymphoma following triple heart bypass surgery – no doubt caused by his sixty-a-day cigarette habit. There's a price to be paid for living life at full tilt - but I'm sure that Simon never wasted a single second.

## Twenty Two

# GIRLS AND CLIENTS

As Black Beauties approached its zenith, I had about twenty hardcore working girls on my books, with a total of sixty in all shapes and sizes and capable of dealing with any predilection. Even though I kept a diary and appointment books (which I still have, along with the books' containing all my clients' details: addresses, phone numbers, monies paid, outstanding bills, cheque stubs, bank receipts, X-rated photos etc., etc.) my life was a whirlwind of clients and girls coming and going and as I ran it all myself, it was hard to keep track.

Sometimes, if a client wanted to book six girls for a party it could get really tricky because everyone was busy with clients. A lot of men liked to have the same girls over and over again. Peggy and Carol remained my most in-demand girls.

Peggy, scatter-brained coke fiend that she was, wasn't bothered whether clients used condoms. Peggy wasn't the sharpest tool in the box but even so, when she got married to a client, a Swedish guy and still wasn't protecting herself on occasions I pointed this out to him, he said he would address it, well, I thought, at least he was told.

Cold-As-Ice-Carol was the perfect hooker in that she had a gorgeous figure and was a pure nymphomaniac. I'd seen her fuck a client at a party without a condom and for free, as she quite liked him and thought it might lead to something more special, which it didn't, then the guy had the nerve to express regret after. She wasn't always the most interactive hooker – she'd often just part her legs and say 'Fuck me.' Despite her coldness and fearlessness, domination wasn't Carol's forte. Nor was it for Peggy – at all. Peggy was like a hippy hooker, a beautiful Naomi Campbell model - in figure and fun to be with - but chaotic. Thank god Peggy didn't ever try crack – it would have been the end of her. The three of us were so different but we enjoyed one another's company.

My other top girls included Adrien, Tina, Veronica, Laura, Christine, Nichola, Margaret (who worked for Cynthia Payne), Bobby, Marie, Shelly, Shani, Sherri (a Trinidadian hairdresser who could get blood out of a stone), Susan, May, Esther, Betty, Kate, Alicia, Dee, Catherine, Claudette, Joan, Jenny, Heather and Loveness (an overweight African drug fiend, (not at the time she worked for me ) here illegally - even after she had a child to a British born guy, she was still deported back to Zambia). Then there was Dana, Charmaine and a woman who later became a university professor, who were my best dominatrices.

Managing them all was a full time job. Christine, whose father was a diplomat, was a beautiful Nigerian girl and privately educated. The guys loved her at first – but she fell into the coke and then crack and I couldn't rely on her. I'd send her on a two-hour booking and she'd stay for 36 hours because the client had coke – the guys in the know ended up getting a very good deal. I kept her on the books for as long as possible, trying to get her to stop using but she wouldn't listen and, after I gave an ultimatum - stop the drugs or leave the agency – she left. This sort of thing wasn't uncommon and meant I had a constant stream of girls going in and out of my big black address book.

I used to have lots of parties, to which I invited clients, my girls as well as friends and acquaintances, everyone in one huge melting pot, but I didn't always get the chance to enjoy them, as I spent most of the time networking and organising hook-ups. Men would take me to one side to arrange to see a girl they liked the look of. They'd think no one else knew what was going on but everyone did – this clandestine behaviour was just part of the fun and I enjoyed being in on everyone's little secrets.

Exhausted, I'd head for my bedroom and lock the door, leaving Charmaine the dominatrix to keep an eye on things. I'd sit with Peggy and Carol or one of my trusted male friends and just chat. Every now and then I'd get disturbed if something got a little out of control. Charmaine once knocked on my door and said: "I think Yvonne's lost her mind."

Yvonne was always quite a flighty and unpredictable girl (the one that ended up moving in with the balding Hague look alike) but even I was surprised to find her in the lounge, on her back in the living room waving her legs and arms in the air, like an insect on its back trying to right itself.

"She's taken ecstasy," Charmaine said.

I was pretty out of it myself and wasn't sure what one did in this kind of situation but one of the men eventually got Yvonne to her feet and helped her to a chair where she sat quietly for a bit, while people chatted around her. I found out some months later that Yvonne had bipolar disorder, by which time she'd moved in with the man who loved to be caned until the skin had been stripped from his bottom.

Ecstasy was everywhere. It had an amazing effect on

Carol in that it turned her into a human being who could joke around and would start talking about her life beyond work. Her personal life wasn't how I imagined it at all. She was so gorgeous, she could have had anyone she wanted but she was married to schoolteacher and they lived together in a house on the outside of central London. This image did not gel with the girl I knew, who would pick up three guys from Stringfellows and fuck them for free, just for the hell of it, but make no mistake Carol was the top earner, mainly because she was also Mr. Twist's golden girl – he absolutely loved her and she was the only girl he ever actually fucked, in the literal sense of the word. He also used to see her on his own in a flat she rented in Holland Park. The only time he ever wrote a cheque was for Carol, when he ran out of cash during an extended session.

Carol's husband knew what his wife did. She eventually left him, buying him out of his share of their house, so she could keep her two Doberman dogs (as she wasn't allowed to keep her dogs in her London flat).

Although Carol came across as being hard as stone, I sometimes had to protect her from the other girls. She simply wasn't into small talk and wasn't easy to get along with - a lot of my girls hated her; there was some jealousy of her looks and her popularity with high-rolling clients.

Despite her beauty and her tough exterior, Carol had some insecurities. She was never really comfortable with her appearance. She had a nose job done at Harley Street all because of a tiny, barely noticeable lump. She was also one of the first people I knew who got into Botox, back then.

Peggy, Carol and I sometimes went together to Stringfellows to let our hair down. I'd arranged with the receptionist, who held the distinction of being one of the first girls to ever appear on Cilla Back's Blind Date, for us to have 'Model Memberships' so we could skip the queue. Stringfellows' door policy was that only the most beautiful girls would be let in and it was nice to be waved in front of the long queue – lots of girls found it difficult to get in.

Once inside we were faced with a constant stream of men trying to pick us up. One night I met a bona fide Texan, hat and all, who, after quickly figuring out what I did, but to be fair most men there thought all girls were available for something or the other. He suggested we meet up later that night, he was staying at the Inn On The Park on Park Lane and he gave me his room number.

"I'm heading off now, but if you want to join me, just come straight up. I'll square things with the doorman."

Never being one to miss an opportunity, once I'd had enough of Stringfellows I took a cab to the hotel but the doorman handed me an envelope with six £50's and a note: 'Sorry, it got too late, but here's my address in the US' – it was Wilshire Boulevard in LA – 'and give me a call if you're ever in town.' I sure will I thought.

The one client we all despaired of was Chris Dowding, whose daughter is Leilani Dowding a former page 3 glamour model, he was so boring. (She recently dated a Hollywood B-List star). Chris loved tall and skinny black girls, the darker the better.

Someone had once told him that he looked like Prince Andrew – there was a slight, if passing resemblance – and he was very proud of the fact, so I told my girls to tell him: "You remind me of someone. Is it Prince Andrew?" They overdid it though as he asked me to tell them to stop doing it a while later, by now suspecting I'd told them to say it.

He was so boring I had to beg girls to see him – even when the price went up. I'd start by saying to Chris: "I've only got one girl who can see you then. She wants £600 for maximum of two hours." He'd agree but I'd still have to plead with them, even after I once got him to £1,500. One thing that sometimes lured the girls in was if lots of coke was available but even when coked out of our brains, being with Chris was like watching paint dry. There was something else as well, something insidious about him, some kind of creeping unpleasantness that infected you over time.

Chris told me he was big in car exhibitions, a high-end car salesman – unfortunately this wasn't a subject girls wanted to talk about for hours at a time. And he loved to talk. Apart from cars, the only other topic he went on and on and on about was his daughter. She was working for a model agency, which we knew to actually be an escort agency, in disguise. There's often a thin line between hooking and modelling.

He wanted the girls to act as if they were in a boyfriend/girlfriend relationship and an evening with Chris would usually include dinner at Crockfords Casino in Mayfair and because he was a big player in the gambling world, he got complimentary food at the casino – and this would include caviar and Dom Perignon. Despite this, he never tipped and so, if I went, I'd make sure to tip the waiters so I'd know I'd be looked after later. This would be followed by gambling, and finally, sex in the small hours – except he wanted to 'make love' and was terrible at it.

Eventually, like a mollusk, he grew firmly attached to one of my girls and he started booking her without calling me. She was kind enough to let me know and I spotted an opportunity. "Do you know what?" I asked Chris, who was by now taking crack as well as coke. "If you pay me £2,500 then you can book her privately and you won't have to pay me any more commission."

Chris thought he'd be better off in the long run without paying agency fees, so agreed. Unfortunately, my celebrations were short-lived as he started calling again once even she got bored with him and left.

*

My life was all work but I lived the work and loved the life. It was exciting; I never knew what each day would bring, whom I would meet or dominate or end up interacting with – even whether with a man or a woman.

I'd sometimes called other agencies for a woman for myself, I was never promiscuous in my private life, but I felt females less intrusive when it came to sex, it became a bit of a habit for a hot minute then I got bored, and stopped. Neither the agencies, nor the girls knew what I did for a living.

I knew how things worked, so gave an exact description of the girls I wanted, essentially blonde and white. It was interesting to see it from the other side, as a customer. The best girls were from gay agencies – they mainly dealt in men but had a few girls on their books. I'd know when some girls had one eye on the clock and I'd know how to get them to refocus on me - with a plentiful supply of cocaine. Once they knew my supply wasn't going to run out, they'd stay long beyond the time I'd booked them for.

It wasn't long, however, before I ended up meeting my beau.

Me hugging Peggy one of the girls that attended
The Bullingdon party hosted my Nathaniel Rothschild

Sonia who had the 'money for sex drama' at Bullindon Party

Mark (king of the yuppies) with a girl, and Carol crashed out from an evening's work!

Hague look alike with Yvonne, they moved in with each other, Geir (ship broker) our relationship started as a paying client then blurred lines occurred and we were boyfriend/girlfriend for a while

## Twenty Three

# MY DATE

In 1992, I was in The Face Restaurant in Chelsea with David and Dana. David was a friend, I knew he fancied me but I wasn't sure yet if he was boyfriend material. We'd met at a nightclub and he'd hung out with my crowd a few times since. Our relationship had been purely platonic one evening he asked me out to dinner. Dana, a mixed-race girl, one of my girls in the Agency, had joined us at the last minute. Dana fancied David but he wasn't into her.

I liked the Face. I knew 'Benny', the owner of the restaurant, quite well, and he always lavished me with attention. We'd just arrived and Benny had come over to say hello when I spotted a young man on another table. He was dark-haired, slim, in his early 20s, wearing a nicely cut suit and tie, and I was instantly attracted to him. He was with some friends, three guys and a couple of girls.

I was trying to concentrate on the company I was in, but I couldn't.

William was one of the most handsome men ever, (still is)

I was intent on saying hi to him, but I couldn't work out if any of the girls were his girlfriend or not. I knew he was aware that I was looking over at him, and my biggest concern was that he would leave before I'd have a chance to speak to him, as his table had ordered their bill.

He got up to go to the loo, and walked passed me, he would return and for sure head straight out the door, only one thing left to do....

"David, can you to do me a favour."

"Sure, what is it?"

"Be a sweetie, you see that guy that just walked by, well he's in the loo, go and tell him I think he's gorgeous. I feel shy doing it myself, let me know what he says." David looked me as though I were mad, then smiled, sighed and said: "Okay."

'Wimp!' I thought. That put me off David straight away. Who would do such a thing without a word of complaint? It was so ridiculous that he did it (but I was grateful, too).

David got up and followed the man to the loo.

Dana also looked at me like I was mad while he was gone.

David was smiling when he got back to the table.

"And?" I asked when David came back. "What did he say?"

"He said he was flattered."

"What else did he say?"

"Nothing, that was it. He sounds like really posh."

At this point, we agreed our date was at an end and David and Dana left me to it. Funnily enough, he and Dana got together after I dismissed him, so perhaps it worked out for the best.

I turned my attention back to this gorgeous man. I wanted him and I was going to have him. He kept looking at me, I smiled when I caught his eye and then beckoned him over.

"Hello," he said. "I'm William."

"Natalie. I'm about to head off to the Bank fancy tagging along??"

A girl, obviously annoyed, followed him over moments later.

"William," she said, "Come on, we've got to go."

"Just a second Tic," William said.

"Excuse me," I said, sensing a rival, "We're talking."

"I don't care," she answered irritably, "We need to leave."

Then a ginger haired young man called Toby joined us.

"Where are you off to?" he asked.

"To the Bank nightclub on the Old Brompton Road," I said. "Why don't you join us?"

They started to debate it, with 'Tic (short for Victoria) against (she obviously fancied the same guy I did) and the boys gradually coming around to my way of thinking as I cajoled them.

As they discussed their plans I leaned over to Tic and whispered in her ear. "Don't get jealous William." He had recently left Bristol University where he'd studied theology and had started a job as a trainee. He came from a wealthy family that was part of the landed gentry. Archibald Sinclair was his grandfather, once the Leader of the Liberal party and was Secretary of State for Air during World War II. His father was Winston Churchill's godson.

None of this I knew, it was his good looks that caught my eye.

Eventually Tic and co left and William joined me and my table, introductions were made, then shortly after we headed off to the club. We had a brilliant night out, got well-oiled on wine and Champagne after that Will came back to my place, he was very mature in mind, his blue eyes telling me he was up for anything, we did a few lines of Charlie and had wonderful sex that night.

Even though I didn't tell him what I did for a living, he was a smart guy with far more experience than most 21-

year-olds and I felt he knew from the first that I was involved in some sort of naughty behaviour

The next morning, William awoke with the mother of all hangovers. I didn't want him to leave.

"What excuse can I give work?"

"Tell them you've got Gastroenteritis and can't get off the loo."

He laughed, I laughed, we both couldn't stop laughing as we rehearsed the telephone call he was to make.

"I'm serious. No one's going to want to go anywhere near you once you tell them that."

William, who loved lavatory humour, had to try and suppress his laughter as he talked to his boss on the phone, trying to sound ill while choking with laughter.

"I'm sorry," he said "But I can't stay away from the toilet, I've got to goooooo!" before hanging up collapsing in a laughing heap on the floor.

We then had the rest of the day together. I loved William from the first. He was smart and funny. When we went to a wine bar for instance and he was merry he would climbed on the table and start to recite poetry or Shakespeare, or anything else he felt inspired to do – he had not the slightest inhibition and I loved it.

I told him he didn't have to go back to work, ever. "Why bother with that crappy job?" So he left and spent more and more time with me.

As for Tic she ended up marrying Viscount (Luke) Bridgeman.

Lots of bookings also came via William's friends. Plenty of them were at Christopher's mews flat near Chelsea football grounds, which he shared with William and Tic, it was Tic' that had purchased it. I sometimes missed not attending some of the parties. It was a shame because these guys were young, energetic and rich and I wanted to be part of the madness – afterwards girls would tell me about all the fun they'd had with them.

Even though William didn't want me to sleep with anyone he knew he eventually admitted to me that he had been intimate with one of my girls, no intercourse apparently, 'but heavy petting' "It was after a party and you'd gone to bed early" he only told me this decades later, when we were no longer in a relationship.

One night I sent Carol, Alysa, Dana and Peggy to attend to seven of William's friends in Queensgate, South Kensington. Alysa was, at 40, the oldest girl on my books, but she looked ten years younger and she loved sex.

They played strip poker and each girl received £450. That was without any sex – that was going to be on top, as they wanted the girls to stay all night. All night was from that evening until 12pm the next day. The girls would call me when they were leaving so I knew until when the client should be billed and when they'd be free for another booking.

All my girls fancied Willie, and I'd always warn the girls before they went on these bookings: "If William's there, hands off".

The problem was, the guys had only booked four girls and there were seven who wanted them, so they decided – after a great many lines of naughties and a great many drinks – that the card game they were playing would change from strip poker to winner-picks-first - and then decides who has whom.

So the winner picked Peggy, allocated Carol to his best friend, presented Alysa to the runner-up and that left Dana. Dana was the least attractive of the bunch, she was pretty just not quite as good a shape as Carol, and others. She was the last to be chosen because she wasn't 'black enough' (she was mixed race). She didn't take kindly to that but luckily, Dana was a true professional – she liked to get in, get the money and get out again, no frills, no time wasted.

But when she went to attend to her client he'd drunk and snorted so much he was no good to anyone and passed out as soon as he laid down. The three men who were left over were so horny that they all wanted Dana, so she called me.

"Is the guy who's passed out still breathing?" I asked, over the phone.

It's always wise to check these things; I was especially conscious ever since Christopher the art dealer had died how easy it was to choke to death on one's own vomit.

"Yes, he's snoring and dribbling."

"Okay make sure he's lying on his side and go ahead and make some money."

Dana left as soon as she was done, followed by Alysa. The girls would always call me when leaving – that way I knew everything was okay and knew I could give them another booking. I always liked to make sure they weren't staying for nothing.

Carol and Peggy both took it upon themselves to stay until mid-afternoon the next day, so they had to pay me an extra fee, even though they hadn't got it from the guys. William's friends were good-looking young guys and my girls just liked going to see them – there was always a good time to be had.

So even though Dana was the last to be picked, she made the most money that night – leaving with four fees (the first client who fell asleep still had to pay), while the more popular girls only had one each and ended up losing some of that for staying on to party the night away.

## Twenty Four

# A LINE, THE BITCH AND A CHANCELLOR

William gave me something I'd longed for, a relationship independent of work, of pleasure for pleasure's sake. I adored him, the way he looked and spoke, his eccentricities (I've often found a certain kind of craziness attractive) and the fact he was up for anything. William and I were born into two different worlds, he in an aristocratic family, Educated at Eton, a trust fund set up for his future, and me, a Comprehensive School, parents immigrants to this wonderful Country, and worked hard for every penny they earned, not spending one day on benefits or handouts from the Government, (Osborne's wet dream). But we clicked and against all odds found each other

He was eight years younger than me but neither of us felt the difference - we were equals. To many people, William and his elite and titled clique were an intimidating bunch. They came from a complex world where background was everything. As Marcel Proust wrote, "everyone at his birth found himself called to that station in life which his parents already occupied."

William once said to me: "I love the fact you're not fazed by us, that we're just normal people to you." It had never occurred to me to treat them any different from anyone else.

Most of them had also been to Eton, except George Osborne which had instilled in them from day one a sense of worldly ownership. I found this innate confidence exceedingly attractive.

William's best friend was Christopher Coleridge, whose father David Coleridge now ex-chairman of Lloyds of London, a direct descendent of Samuel Taylor Coleridge and brother of Nicholas, the owner of the Conde Nast magazine empire. Their friendship dated back to Eton.

Chris, with a Mr. Bean/upper-class appearance, looked like the archetypal toff - although he always did his best not to give the impression he was a multi-millionaire. He drove cheap second-hand cars but once went to a Knightsbridge estate agents and asked them to find him a home for £2million. When they showed him what was available and nothing took his fancy, he soon jumped up to £5million, without any hesitation, so much for trying to live as a humble man. I'll give him a little credit at that stage in his life he was buying a marital home. He was always kind and considerate and although he was the richest of William's close friends, he tended to be a little tight in the pocket area... at least when it came to the naughties.

Chris met George Osborne while at Oxford; they were both members of the infamous Bullingdon Club. By the time I had started seeing William, the three of them were close friends and often turned up at my place together. I called them my 'Three Musketeers'. I nick named them, William was 'Willie Wonka', George was 'Georgie Porgy' and Chris was 'Christopher Robin'.

George first arrived at my place in Prince of Wales Terrace with Chris, along with his friend Philip Delves Broughton, a writer for the New York Times. George was an attractive 22-year-old and it was immediately clear that girls considered him to be highly eligible – they were always vying for his attention. I thought he was quite good-looking, (back then) but much preferred William.

At this time George didn't show any signs of the defiant or deviant character, he went on to display as Chancellor of the Exchequer, although he did have a complete dislike for the unemployed even back then, he was very impressed by the fact that the Cocaine dealer, whom he got on very well with, had put himself through University without any financial assistance, although by proxy George was contributing to the dealers income from all the Cocaine he and his pals were buying, if only in a small way. Chris and William and others teased him about his background, (his father is the co-founder of Osborne & Little, the fabric and wallpaper designers) in essence an high end shop, and the fact he wasn't an Etonian, although it hasn't bothered Prime Minster David Cameron, George took it without complaint; he had this 'look' he would give me that said 'How pathetic are they?' ignore them, George was very thick skinned criticism was not something he took any notice of.

Despite the fact that they all came from incredibly wealthy families, they always argued about money, everything from splitting a restaurant bill to who was paying for what from the off license, to who had snorted more cocaine than the other, Chris never brought cash with him and usually ended up writing a cheque out to George or William, or me, to cover the cash for the coke. It was amazing to see them arguing about a three-way split over a meal. George was the most relaxed and acted as mediator, especially when it came to the cocaine, he'd make sure everyone paid their fair share, and as William was rather greedy when it came to the coke, George kept a beady eye on him. At some point in our sessions, someone re named cocaine 'naughties', from then on that was the new code word.

They also came up with strategies to save money in restaurants. I once watched as they ordered the waiter to bring them bottles of both red and white wine, as they weren't sure which they wanted with their meal. They drank both bottles and told the waiter they were only going to pay for one.

The waiter raised his eyebrows. "But you've had both bottles."

"Each of us had to taste it. By that time it was empty."

Sure enough, the bottle was removed from the bill. They liked to provoke people deliberately – it reassured them when they got a result that confirmed the power of their social class.

Whenever the three of them were together with me, we were ourselves; it was as if the usual pressures and rivalries brought about by their privileged family backgrounds didn't exist.

It was fun to see these young boys, experimenting with life and enjoying themselves. Occasionally, especially during drinking games (William always won; he had to win everything), we ran out of booze. There was a 24-hour shop with an off-license at the end of the road whose owners were prepared to ignore the 11pm license so we could buy alcohol at any time (as long as we were prepared to pay double the ticket price) but even after the boys had settled the arguments about who was going to pay what, they'd argue about who was going to go and get it. Once the boys had had a few glasses of wine down them they could unwind, then as the merriment got under way it was time for a line or two! I would chop up the lines equally for whom ever wanted one which was everyone, 'come on boys its ready! then I'd roll up a note and give it to them, George and Christopher usually used a £ note, but because William tended to nose bleed, I would roll up a piece of paper for his use, no one seemed that bothered but I was. The minute George Osborne snorted a line up his nostrils he was in John Travolta mode, not the best dancer I've ever come across but what he lacked in technique he certainly made up in gusto. George after having a line of cocaine transformed into a more carefree almost naughty school boy, he became less serious and frankly couldn't get enough of the stuff up his eager nostrils. I don't think he could ever let his hair down as freely in his other life as much as when he came round to my place for our drug and alcohol fuelled party.

When the booze ran out, I'd toss a coin as to who went to the shop, I sometimes cheated and made sure George didn't lose, as it gave me a buzz that he and I knew, because unknown to William, we'd exchange a wink and knowing look because he knew what I was doing.

On one particularly drunken evening at my flat in Prince of Wales Terrace, I made a bet with George, Chris and William that they would strip off naked, run out the door, down the street to a building that was fifty metres away and back again. The first one back would get a 'prize'.

Eventually, after a bit of cajoling, the three of them agreed, stripped off completely starkers and waited by the front door.

"Ready?" I said, my hand on the door handle. "Set... Go!"

I threw open the door and off they ran down the front steps, bottoms wobbling as they pounded down the street.

And, of course, I locked the door and went back inside.

I watched as they came running back, cheering them on. They all arrived more or less at the same time and couldn't believe what I'd done to them.

"Please let me back in!" the future Chancellor of the Exchequer pleaded.

They all begged, hands over their willies, and I just watched, laughing. I laughed so much that I rolling on the floor and thought I might even wee myself. Luckily for them, my building was in a quiet cul-de-sac.

I gave them a good few minutes, which must have seemed like hours, god knows what any passer-by would have made of three naked men standing in the street. Finally, when I'd decided they'd had enough, I let them back in.

They loved it and were all laughing afterwards – they'd enjoyed the joke.

The three musketeers were proper little ravers and loved to go clubbing. They all were terrible dancers, I used to cringe when we went clubbing with the three musketeers and their friends. I couldn't bring myself to share the dance floor with them – the one thing that mummy and daddy's money couldn't buy was rhythm. The higher they got, the better they thought they were.

George loved We Could Be Heroes by David Bowie and the three musketeers would sing it together top of their voices on the dance floor. George also adored Gold by Spandau Ballet. George didn't have much of dress sense, neither did he make an effort to dress up – he just wore jeans and T-shirt. William usually wore a suit and tie and occasionally a polo shirt and jeans. The three of them had very different music tastes to me - William drove me mad listening to the same Elvis records over and over again, although he had an half decent voice.

# THE PHOTOGRAPH

The photograph with the cocaine for all to see! The right of the vase on a table mat, with an unravelling piece of white paper

On one of my gatherings at my home in Redcliffe Sq., the boys came round. I had only moved in a matter of months prior. Robin had come round earlier that day for a session. After it had ended he hung around as he sometimes did.

I told him that William, Chris, and George were coming by and he was eager to say hi, the boys by now were used to hanging out with some of my clients, so it was nothing unusual to see Robin when they arrived.

I was 3 months pregnant so was unable to part take in the booze and drug session that was about to ensue. The boys were in high spirits and ready for their 'naughties' to arrive. There was a little coke left over from Robin' session so they had some of his, till the dealer arrived.

On came the music out came the bottles of wine and we all sat around discussing our day.

Robin and William were polishing up on their Russian

between themselves, I was always impressed that Will could speak Russian fluently.

George was entering the life of Politics, at the time and showed no signs to me that he had his eye on the big prize, running the Economy.

The cocaine arrived, the dealer hung around as they do, waiting for the gear to run out, to save them a trip coming back, which was more the case than not. The boys loved mingling with people that were not of their ilk -, not upper class. They'd sometimes even play games of who could do the best cockney accent, they all sounded ridiculous. I as I did on many occasions, took care of chopping up the Coke and making the lines.

I placed it on a table mat as it was easier to pass round, and less damage to my dining table, and the boys took their turns in taking a line.

At some point I decided to take some photographs on my camera, everyone took turns in posing for me and at some point I passed the camera for some shots of me with the boys, could be taken.

George was sat beside me around the dining table, I divided a line of cocaine and he took a big fat line.

Before the picture was taken with me and George, I was mindful that the cocaine was on the table, and I didn't want the camera to pick it up. So I strategically moved the vase (I thought) in front of the coke that was on the table mat, there was a rolled up piece of white paper besides the coke that William had used to snort with, because he would sometimes nose bleed, instead of bleeding all over the money £notes. I thought that the camera wouldn't have picked up the cocaine in front of me and George but it fortunately or unfortunately did. After he took a line he was ready to compete in Flash Dance, that was when he really came out of his shell as did the others also, they'd sing, dance, just have a wild time in general. It was a fun time, watching them let their hair down. At some point in the evening the subject came up on politics, after George had taken another line. I jokingly said to him "when your Prime Minster one day, I'll have all the goods on you", he knew that meant more than him doing cocaine. He laughed, I laughed and the evening carried on.

*

I experienced racism first hand when we went to a party at Chris's parents' house, which was in a quiet Knightsbridge cul-de-sac where houses sell for tens of millions.

One girl handed me a melon quarter and tried to make out I was a monkey and another young man (a Bullingdon Club member, Mark now deceased), made monkey noises behind my back. I was furious but didn't kick off because I didn't want to embarrass William. I was the only black person there and William was already getting a hard time because he was seeing a black girl – and it seemed that word had spread that I ran an escort agency.

Some party-goers picked on my friend Pierre. Pierre was a gay French drug dealer who I'd met at the Face nightclub – he liked to hang out with us because it meant he'd have plenty of chances to meet posh young men. The fact that Pierre was picked on only made me angrier – especially as I knew that a lot of the men there were taking dildos up their arses anyway.

By the time I was cornered by a tall, self-righteous blonde girl, I was ready to explode.

"Don't you feel guilty about how you make a living?" She asked in a bitchy voice, looking down her nose. "You know, destroying relationships."

"On the contrary, I save relationships. You look familiar. Isn't your father Lord X?"

"Yes, he is as a matter of fact."

"Well, he's been fucking me for years now, so shut your mouth."

I walked off, leaving her with her jaw hanging open.

The only reason I didn't punch someone was because I didn't want to let William down. I really did feel out of place at this party. I'd never really felt that way before as with my clients I always felt on a par - and I was with them at my home and on my terms.

It annoyed me that the three musketeers stood by and said nothing while the rest of their set ridiculed gay and black people.

I did get an apology once we left the party, although William told me "It's not such a big deal. There was one black boy at Eton and everyone called him Golly and he accepted it as perfectly normal."

Chris sent me some flowers the next day. Although George never once said anything like: "I really hate what they're saying," at the time (I suppose he thought he'd be better off saving his energy – there was no chance of him making them stop), he was the most upset of the three and this made me feel close to him.

When we were alone George told me he couldn't understand why I was with William; he said we just weren't compatible.

I knew that George had the hots for me, he said that he'd wished he'd met me before William, I was pretty hot back then so it was no surprise how he felt.

*

I'd sometimes have parties at my place and thirty or forty people would come. Everyone got on well together – the posh ones tended to congregate, as did the City boys. Not all the girls were working girls, some were friends I'd met at clubs and through clients – I was sociable and liked to 'collect' people.

At this time Thatcherism was triumphant, there was so much money around and the bars and clubs were full of energy - which meant these were also the golden years for hookers.

After I left Rudi I was living the life, and boy did I party! I met and very briefly dated Mark Fielding (born Mark Rennie), whom the News of the World gave him the accolade and crowned "King of the Yuppies." When the 1991 recession hit, his attitude was: "Fuck 'em, it's a win-win for us brokers, suckers invest their money if they lose they lose, so long as I don't." He once joked that he had to call a client to tell him all his investment had gone, I asked Mark if he felt guilty, he replied "no, I couldn't give a shit if he jumped out of a high building", it made it clear to me that the only people that lose out when the banks screw up are, the investors never the bank, as current events such as bailing out the banks demonstrate. 'got money to lose, then that's their problem.' He was a broker in the city, but at some point he was struck off and then pursued a more fraudulent career. We only went out for a short time and later in the Years to come Mark ended up in prison for fraud, in 2001 after he conned about 1,500 people by promising to employ them as international couriers. He charged them a registration fee and a further fee that would allow them to fly business class. He just took their money (about £60k altogether) and disappeared abroad.

Even the recession didn't slow things down – the crowd I hung around with certainly didn't care about anyone who was suffering economic hardship and they remained unscathed.

Some brokers how ever did fall by the way side and one of them was my client Harald, whom I had many fantastic adventures with all over the world, he was from Norway, a stockbroker and recovering alcoholic, who was exposed as an embezzler. His wife left him soon after this (she caught him with a hooker). I saw Harald a many years later when a Norwegian friend Stig and I visited Norway, Harold by now had moved back to Norway, so as I was in the country I popped in to say 'hello'. Harald had been a strapping mature man and at first I didn't recognise the shuffling decrepit who opened the front door. Inside there were hundreds of bottles everywhere – he'd not thrown away a single bottle for a year. It was clear he was dying before my eyes. Harald wanted me to stay but couldn't bring myself to; I made my excuses and left. He died a short time later, having had a triple by-pass and a raving alcoholic, a heart attack was inevitable, and he had a fatal one.

Everyone seemed to be taking ecstasy at this time. The high from a line of coke would last 3-4 minutes and then subside. With E you could be 'up' for an hour or more. Amazingly I've never tried one, I much preferred coke but Peggy, bless her, would try anything at least once. At one of my parties I found her high on E in my bathroom with two of William's friends.

"Peggy! What do you think you're doing?"

Peggy just shrugged.

"Right you two, you're taking advantage. If you want to have sex with Peggy, you're going to have to pay." Sure enough, they coughed up the cash and I left them to it.

I went and sat with George on the sofa. George couldn't hold his own in conversation with his peers, which is why we ended up talking a lot together – we would share the fact that we didn't have a clue, nor were we interested in what the others were going on about – arts, politics and the social shenanigans of the landed gentry. Obvious to me now that George did have an interest in politics but was keeping that card very near to his chest.

We were passing comment on somebody at the party when I leant over to whisper something to him and playfully licked his ear. William appeared. He'd seen what was going on and was pissed off.

"What are you guys talking about?" he asked angrily.

"Calm down William," George said. "You're letting your paranoia get the better of you."

The argument escalated quickly. When George tried to stand up William pushed him back down into the sofa. George then made a grab for William and they started tussling with one another. As I leapt out of the way the sofa tipped over and they rolled out onto the floor, still fighting – although it was the grappling-and-rolling type rather than the punching-and-kicking kind of fight. I thought it was hilarious.

"Come on, stop it, this is ridiculous!"

By the time they'd calmed down and made up, nobody had thrown a punch.

I saw the three musketeers every weekend. One popular haunt was Wall Street Nightclub, in Mayfair, It was jam packed with bankers, trust fund kids with more money that they could ever spend in a life time, maybe it was the clubs name that attracted all the city brokers. We'd usually go to the VIP section upstairs, where pop stars, actors and the upper classes filled the private rooms - where you could get away with pretty much anything.

I met Prince the singer musician there, and once bumped into Bobby Brown, who went on to marry the singer Whitney Houston, He had just made a fool of himself by falling off the stage at the MTV music awards and I asked him what had happened.

"I bust my butt," was all he would tell me, clearly off his trolley on something. He wasn't very friendly but that wasn't perhaps the best question to ask him.

On another occasion I was dating a beautiful, very well-built guy called Jez, while propping up the bar a man planted himself between us with his back to me, and It was George

Michael the singer, he proceeded to try and chat up Jez, who would have nothing to do with him, I was just pleased to be propping up the bar alongside the talented George Michael.

Osborne just after he'd snorted some cocaine, now in John Travolta mode!

William and George feeling GOOD!

## Twenty Five

# MORE LINES, A BITCH AND A CHANCELLOR

One day William came round when longstanding slave Robin was with me. I was bored with Robin so he was now paying me thousands per session, to keep me interested. He had all the traits of dear Christopher Hewitt who had died so tragically, in a time in my life that was so different from the one I was now living, I sometimes humoured myself with the idea that Christopher had sent Robin in his place by proxy, as Robin was pretty much a replica in his behaviour By now I knew quite a lot about Robin Whitby, but the one thing he seemed to evade giving me a straight answer to, was what he did for a living all though I knew all about him – his children and wife – he never revealed what his job was. Every now and again, there'd be a 'mishap' where he'd end up with a bruise or two. Once he had a bruised eye, goodness knows how he explained that to his wife. On this evening he asked: "Can we be careful Mistress?"

"Why is that?"

"Tomorrow I have an appointment at Downing Street with Tony Blair." What that meeting was about was any bodies guess, "really" I said. "What's it about?" "Can't say"

I got the feeling that he had regretted mentioning it at all, maybe he was showing off, I pressed further but he kept tight lipped.

In the beginning Robin had enquired about my new boyfriend William and was a little jealous, he wanted to meet William so I, showing of myself my handsome beau, and at the same time making Robin feel even more inadequate, I said he could meet Will but to pretend to be my accountant, well! All I can say is that, our little plan didn't last more than 20 minutes from the time they both met. The dynamics between me and Robin was as clear to any idiot, anyone could see that he wasn't my accountant, and William was no fool. So having gone on with the stupid idea for a hot minute, I told William the truth that Robin was into S&M games, now with great relief the cat was out of the bag. The fact that Robin called me Mistress (I think on purpose) and our session had been over at least an hour before William arrived didn't help matters, plus he was snorting up a line like no tomorrow – so I had to explain it to William.

He took it in his stride as he was a broad minded soul.

I asked William to keep it to himself and he did - until the day I left the three musketeers in my flat while I went off to score some charlie, for the guys weekly session of fun, naughties and dance.

I'd left out the gear – the whip, Robin's favourite dog collar and lead – and my outfit - 6-inch heels fishnets and tight leather skirt – when the doorbell rang. It was George, Chris and William.

I let them in and told them to wait, forgetting about the domination gear. When I got back William was pretending to whip George, while Chris was sword fighting with the cane.

"What's all this Nat?" Chris asked.

I smiled. Confession time. "I'm a dominatrix."

They were impressed. "Tell us what you get up to!"

So I told them some of my adventures with my clients. They bombarded me with questions.

"So how much do you charge?" George asked me, rather keenly.

"It depends on a few things, on their pain threshold, how much work is involved, and so on but there's a basic rate to start."

They loved to hear what was going on and I enjoyed telling them. They certainly hadn't met anyone like me before.

Some of my clients whom I'd known for a long time like John would hang around after we'd finished, I had mentioned to John about William and his pals, John who worked in the Lloyd of London building said he knew Christopher' father, John was intrigued about the chairman's son's activities.

So John eventually met up with the boys, they'd chat together, well it was more of an interrogation of John into what he got up to, pain threshold, outfits he wore those boys didn't let up, they soaked up every last detail. George really enjoyed this; it was as if he was sharing in their experience with me. George and the Lloyd's of London executive would enjoy copious amounts of cocaine while talking shop about investments and the economy all of which went right over my head!

\*

Then one day the inevitable happened George asked privately if he could experience what I did to those that liked a bit of S&M, I wasn't surprised at all, I kind of

184

expected it, has he seemed to always want that extra detail more so than Christopher or any of the others. He had popped round to my flat on his own on a few occasions to score some Cocaine, and we would chat about what I'd got up to with my slaves that day or previously. I was always happy to see George, he wasn't a bad looker in those days, and I knew he liked me a lot. We once had a little snog at one of my parties both of us high on charlie, after he told me he'd never been intimate with a black before, never had the opportunity before, I jokingly said that once you've experienced me you'll want more!

He then asked me if I would consider it, I made it clear to George that our relationship would have to be strictly professional, and that meant he would have to pay.

"Of course," he said, "I understand."


The lounge was upstairs, the two bedrooms were downstairs and the windows had metal bars. In case there was an unexpected visitor and George needed to make a discrete exit, the plan was George would leave through the fire exit from my bedroom conveniently located alongside a walk-in wardrobe.

I explained how every client had a safe word, which he had already learned from all the past drilling from a couple of my clients, namely Robin and John, then I'd stop and end the session. George chose 'Louise' I had no idea why he chose that particular safe word and it didn't matter.

He didn't ask how much; he already knew my rate. When we went downstairs to the bedroom he put the money on a side table - £350.

The first session wasn't like a normal domination session. It was more sexual with a little bit of pain involved.

We undressed. He was very turned on. He kissed my feet and toes, and proceeded to pleasure me, at some point

I put the nipple clamps on George and tightened them until he couldn't help himself and cried out.

"Don't make a sound. If you even moan I'm going to slap you."

He moaned.

I slapped his face. "You're pathetic!" He showed that he was nervous, and had a little smirk, I told him to "take the smirk off his face"

I made him snort some coke and allowed him to suck some off my nipples. We then got more intimate, with just a touch of firmness from me about what he should do, he didn't have much rhythm, he came across very inexperienced in regards to sex.

Even though he wanted me to try out the domination on him, I did at first wonder whether it was to please me or whether he liked it. I was itching to 'perform' and show him what I was capable of – but he had to be the one to decide how far he wanted to go – there was no set menu, I had to be attentive to what my clients said, and never second guess them. I decided I would make each session a little more extreme and see how far George was prepared to go.

During the next session I got the impression he couldn't quite believe he was doing what he was doing. He was also really surprised at how I was able to switch into this very different person. It would have been even more awkward without the coke to release his inhibitions.

"Tell me how much you love and adore me," I'd demand as he sucked my heels and licked my shoe.

The pain was not sexually arousing for him. The majority of times slaves do not come – domination is, most of the time, more of a mind-fuck than a body-fuck.

It was tricky with George because he was a friend, and moreover, Williams friend. If William found out he would have punched his lights out. George would be fucked, much more than me. There were only a handful of clients that got to know me on a personal level, but even then, once the role play begun, we kept in that Zone till it was over. One man told me he had to stop seeing me because, after we'd chatted for a while, he said I reminded him of his daughter, in personality. And I felt relieved too, because he was just 'too nice' now for me to treat as a slave.

Taking money from George to preform was awkward and confused things slightly as I was a hooker to him now, as well as a friend. But at the same time money helped control the situation – he had paid for my services and he was a slave for the duration – not a friend. He placed the cash it on the bedside table with a slight awkwardness.

Our sessions became more intense each time. Eventually we reached the stage where George put on a collar, got on all fours and became my little dog. I'd command him to bark and pant as he crawled around the room. If he wasn't barking enough, he'd get a paddle on the bottom, he wore a black pair of rubber pants, that would limit the bruising, (didn't always work depended how hard I hit a client) he liked being submissive, it seemed to me. Then I made satisfy me, after I was satisfied I allowed him to get on his knees and wank until he came while I tightened the nipple clamps. After it was over, we had some lines of coke, went upstairs and carried on with our day.

As a slave for a madam, he was a 4 out of 10. And I don't mean this as an insult, just that he wasn't that kind of guy, he wasn't a proper slave – he wasn't good at handling pain for a start. But he wasn't shy and if he didn't like it I'm sure he wouldn't have done it again – we saw each other in this secret manner on a few occasions while living at Prince of Wales Terrace.

Once he'd changed into whatever he had to wear that session – rubber pants or dog collar - we began. We'd take cocaine during the whole performance.

He only used the safe word once.

We both found it exciting after our sessions, when we met up among friends – we had a silent understanding, our dirty secret.

I really liked George but William was more interesting to me, I always knew it wasn't forever – he was my bit on the side. He didn't have William's charisma, good looks and craziness. It all stopped before I fell pregnant to William, and then I only saw George socially the George Osborne I knew back then is how I'll always remember him, on all fours getting his arse trashed, pay back in lieu of the havoc he now dishes out on the vulnerable people in our society.

The first time I fell pregnant to William I didn't think it was the right time to battle the risks again to try to have a baby. I also hadn't been seeing William that long and was still running Black Beauties, which had never been busier. Nigel, the old Etonian who'd been my longest serving and most faithful slave, was so desperate for me to continue seeing him that he offered me money not to have the child – an offer I declined, but I didn't go through with the pregnancy for my own reasons. I was depressed afterwards and William noticed this. He's a very religious man and I think he felt guilty about encouraging me to have the abortion, although it was my decision so things were different when I fell pregnant again just six months later. I decided that perhaps God was trying to tell me something and decided this time I was going to be a mum.

This time when I told William, he said: "Do what you feel is right for you. If you want to have the child it's fine with me."

Then it was time to tell Nigel. Our relationship had become more serious through the years – our sessions had progressed from domination to having sex – and I'd been in love with him throughout. He was the closest thing I had to a boyfriend until I met William.

When I told Nigel I was planning to have William's baby he again asked me to have an abortion.

We'd often talked together about what I would do if I stopped hooking and I had mentioned I was interested in studying psychology with a view to becoming a counsellor or therapist

Nigel told me that if I had an abortion then he would set me up with my own practice and would pay for everything. "You'll have your dream business and will never have to worry about money, and we can still see one another. Then, if you still want a child, let me give it to you."

I was appalled. People think that because you're a hooker, you always have a price when this isn't the case at all. Hooking was a job and I charged people for it. Nigel was effectively saying that he was prepared to pay me to kill my child. Only I could make that decision. I knew my life would change but I wasn't getting any younger and I was ready. I had a good feeling about this pregnancy and I wanted to see it through. No one, no matter what they offered me, could ever buy that decision from me.

Nigel made this offer because he was scared he was going to lose me, and perhaps I hadn't realised fully just how much had I meant to him, or I'd lost sight of the unusual foundations of our relationship. Whatever the case, Nigel wanted to own me, so it seemed as though his ancestral slave trader blood still ran thick.

The next major change for me was to stop hooking. This had an immediate financial and social impact on my life. Shortly after I made my decision to try and have William's baby, I received a phone call from another hooker who was out in Monaco with Mr. Twist. Mr. Twist wanted some girls from Black Beauties, she said, and, if I could send some over, her pimp would sort out my commission.

It isn't easy to get good-looking girls with the right figure and who could travel abroad at short notice. A lot of hookers are here illegally. One Nigerian girl who was here illegally had managed to get a fake passport in the name of Baker, so I sent her, along with the girl who later became a university professor. I would have gone too, had I not been pregnant.

Once they got there, the pimp gave them £3,000 each as their basic fee.

"Don't worry, you'll get your cut later on," he told me over the phone, "Once I'm back in London."

I didn't, so I went to see the pimp and the prostitute. She lived in an apartment in Chelsea Cloisters in Sloane Avenue. These apartments used to be available for short-term-lets. They were expensive, but as long as you paid the hefty deposit, you could stay as long as you needed, no questions asked, no references required. Hookers and celebrities used them all the time.

I once stayed in one of the serviced apartments in Nell Gwynn House, further down Sloane Avenue, while I was moving between my flats in Prince of Wales Terrace and Redcliffe Square. Mr. Twist used these apartments as well, as you could rent them by the day.

When I got there, the pimp was waiting and even though I was pregnant, he had no trouble threatening me. There was nothing I could do and so lost £17k in commission. If I'd been able to travel to Monaco and had seen Mr. Twist, I probably would have managed to get my commission. Running an agency like mine requires total commitment, energy and Balls with a capital B. Being pregnant made my job that much harder to do.

My pregnancy also changed the dynamics between me and my three musketeers. George became quite caring towards me. He'd sometimes cosy up to me in my flat on the sofa in Redcliffe Square and rub my pregnant tummy – even when other people were there, we had our little secret, well… until now.

George was always self-conscious of his figure, he struggled with his weight – he would wear loose clothes to try and hide his belly, which was a bit flabby and spongy. He had a favourite grey woolly jumper that he liked to wear a lot, has it hid he chubby tummy. Every now and then I'd comment: "Why are you wearing this? To hide your jelly-belly?" and would reach over and rub it playfully.

George Osborne and William - high on drugs and alcohol.
Robin (client) watches them in amusement.

## Twenty Six

# THE BULLINGDON CLUB

I never personally witnessed George Osborne bedding any of my girls although he certainly attended some of the parties that I sent my girls to.

The Bullingdon is an all-male dining/drinking club founded in the 1780s. Members are selected from the most ennobled and wealthiest Oxford University undergraduates (former members include Edward VIII, David Cameron and Boris Johnson) and the club's members are infamous for their loutish behaviour. Members are sworn to secrecy, although the Observer Magazine managed to interview one of George Osborne's Bullingdon contemporaries who (on condition of anonymity) detailed "an alcohol-fuelled party that degenerated into a fist fight, allegations of cocaine use by another member of the club, and an evening during which the members trashed a Michelin-starred restaurant."

New members have to buy the uniform, at a cost of £3,500. It's still in the same ridiculous fashion now as it was in 1780: navy tailcoat, mustard waistcoat, sky-blue silk bow tie and brass buttons. It's brought out for private dinners held in rural hotels or in family estates in the Oxford countryside - as well as for the annual photograph.

When it was revealed that David Cameron and Boris

Johnson had both been members, thanks to one these annual members' photographs leaking into the public domain, and then that the duo had engaged in some pretty riotous behaviour while members, Cameron responded:

'We all do stupid things when we are young and we should learn the lessons,'

This was in 2011, in an interview with the BBC's Evan Davis. Cameron then went on to attack the behaviour of the London rioters of that summer.

Some would say, as Davis pointed out, that the electorate would be hard pushed to tell the difference between the behaviour of a 'Buller' and the rioters.

My experience of the Bullingdon crowd confirms this view.

One evening at one of my evenings of entertaining George, William, and Christopher, I was asked if I could arrange 3 of my best girls to attend their annual Bullingdon Club gatherings, I was only too happy to oblige.

I didn't know anything at the time as to what this Bullingdon Club was all about, only that it was basically all their chums getting together and raving it up.

The request was for the body type of Naomi Campbell or as close to as possible, the girls were to, after arriving, get dressed into bra, knickers, high heels and suspenders to do a striptease - with "benefits", plus I was to make sure one of the girls bought the cocaine, with her. Easily done. I couldn't go, as I was in the early stage of my pregnancy and even if I had been able, I certainly would only have gone as a voyeur, there's no way for many reasons that I would ever strip in front of a group of Williams pals, (he wouldn't have allowed it anyway) 2nd I prefer to work in a less exposed situation. I sent Peggy, Carol, and Sonia. Carol drove the girls down in her brand new red convertible 5 series BMW, the result of one night's work for Mr. Twist.

The girls arrived at Waddesdon Manor, the host was Nathaniel Rothschild, the boys just called him Nat. The last member of the Rothschild family to own Waddesdon was James de Rothschild, now it's in the hands of the National Trust. Carol called me to say things were going well, brilliant! I thought, I told her who to give the coke to, I had already been paid in advance for the stuff. (non-members who were blue-blooded enough, could attend, that included William, he didn't go to Oxford and therefore wasn't an official member of the Bullingdon Elite. William, George and Chris were there to look after my girls I thought, but at some point the occasion started to get out of hand and not even my three Musketeers could control the Bullingdon mob.) The evening had started well, the girls had been dancing on tables in their get up and the boys loved it, but as they drank more and more and took more and more cocaine, a few of the boys lost control and started racially abusing the girls, wanting to cop a feel, the rules were no touching without payment in advance, this had already been made clear prior. I had got a call from Carol and she was not happy at all, "They're behaving like wild animals that have never seen a female before" she was beside herself, "put William on the phone" I told her, after I'd spoken to Will that the posh thugs would now behave, but oh! no!, I'd presumed wrong. Even William couldn't control the wild drunken coked to high heaven toffs. After the girls had finished their striptease, ripped panties to boot, after one member didn't think they were stripping fast enough for his liking, it was time for the negotiations as to who was going to fuck who. – one row broke out after one prominent young millionaire (he knows who he is) had his sexual urge fulfilled courtesy of Sonya, then decided that he would only pay £100, the tight little shit, that caused a row, I was called again, I made it very clear that if I had to come down there he would have no balls left to use in the future, He soon coughed up the £350 that had been agreed. Other Bullingdon boys had the delights of my Black Beauties, whether George did I don't know, Christopher did no surprise there has I had sent him girls before on past occasions, he got a slight discount being best pal of William' and as far as I'M AWARE, William kept his in is pants!

William told me he'd tried to calm the few troublesome boys down but things got worse, the girls decided to leave, but some of the bullying thugs thought different, Carol especially had had enough and just wanted to leave, Peggy was having a romp somewhere on the grounds, and I insisted that she shouldn't leave without her, as long as there was Coke around Peggy would practically move in. Eventually Carol tracked Peggy down, all three of the girls now headed for the car. The bully boys thought different, and a few gathered in the path way in front of Carol' car and surrounded her, a few decided they would sit on the bonnet of her brand new car, they were now jeering and banging the roof and started rocking her brand new BMW from side to side, until it felt to Carol as though they were going to tip it over onto its side. Fortunately, she had a car phone and dialled 999 - the police arrived minutes later.

The police were in awe of all these rich, spoiled Oiks; although they took statements from everyone, no one was arrested despite the near riot conditions and obvious drug taking by some members of the club, and the police had to persuade the boys to let the girls leave (they wanted to carry on the party).

Basically the Cops had their nose' stuck right up the posh boys arses. When I later met up to collect my fee, which worked out to at least 5 guys that had paid for 'extras', all but Peggy said they would never go to a Bullingdon gathering ever again. Except for Peggy, who was meeting up the following week for lunch with one of them, who she really thought was hot, hmm! I thought I bet lunch won't be at mummy's.

Every year, an official photograph is taken of the members of the Bullingdon Club. The most famous ones, from 1992 and 1993, have been widely published and feature George Osborne, Chris Coleridge and Nathaniel Rothschild – but the 1994 photo has never surfaced, presumed destroyed for fear of the scandal it might cause if my girls, with whom I'm still in touch, started pointing out the famous faces they'd fucked, along with any other crimes and misdemeanours. David Cameron could well be in the now tucked away 1994 pic, or maybe my girls could answer that question!

## Twenty Seven

# JOHN WHITTINGDALE
# Conservative MP

John Whittingdale should resign!

Around November 2013 a source came to me with information that John Whittingdale was having a relationship with a known prostitute who specialised in S&M. (Whose name I've chosen not to reveal at this present time).

The vice girl worked in a well-established basement flat in Central London.

I then gave the story (with the permission of my source) to a tabloid Newspaper.

The woman in question was using cocaine on a daily basis and had extreme alcohol abuse issues.

Was he using public money in order to pay for a home that he had set her up in? Had he claimed expenses on official business that he had taken her to? These were just a few questions among many that needed to be investigated.

But what happened after I gave the story to a tabloid is most sinister.

I was told it was potentially a story that could possibly cause Whittingdale to resign.

All I was to do was to relay his movements with her to

the journalist that was overseeing the story at the paper.

My source then started giving me information as to when Whittingdale and the prostitute would meet up and places they would be going to.

We already knew that he had taken her to the X FACTOR talent show finals in Amsterdam and that he was in the process of taking her to a Royal event.

So every time I received any info I then relayed it back.

So on the day he was to attend the annual Sports Ball in 2013, I informed the paper that he would be taking her with him.

He was on official business as he was the Culture Media and Sports Committee Chairman. The idea was to get photos of Whittingdale and the Hooker attending together.

The photographer was notified and he indeed got the pics the paper wanted.

This was a huge event as Kate Middleton- The Duchess of Cambridge was the guest of honour as she is the Patron of SportsAid.

The photographer also had both Whittingdale the hooker on video as they left the Sports Ball, to go back to his home. The hooker in question- while at the event was relaying everything back to a 'friend' of hers by text message.

What's worrying is that she could have been a security risk apart from a political embarrassment for Whittingdale.

The paper also had a video of them at the X FACTOR finals London, in the same year.

It was all looking good for the paper to get set.

But what I didn't know was that someone at the paper was already tipping John Whittingdale off about the fact that my source was trying to sell a story on the Conservative MP and his hooker.

John Whittingdale then notified her of what he knew.

She then unwittingly told my source that someone was trying to sell a story on her and Whittingdale.

The irony of it was she said (to my source) she didn't want to end up being the next 'Miss Whiplash' (referring to me, a phrase the tabloids titled me with)

I was mortified.

I relayed what I'd been made aware of and was assured that there wasn't a leak at the papers.

John Whittingdale then took her to see the fireworks display at The Houses of Parliament to see in the New Year. She also gave out her 'business cards' to other members of Parliament that attended the do.

Then the bombshell came!

She told my source that Whittingdale had shut down any story about him and her and that no paper would run the story, that he had his own source at the very paper that I had given my story to.

Whittingdale then proceeded to educate her on what she should do if any press were to approach her; she was to call the Press Complaints and he coached her on exactly what to say. And she did indeed put a call in to the Press Complaints department.

He was now abusing his power as the Secretary of State for Culture and media, the papers didn't want to upset him and he knew that.

Most of the papers wanted self-regulation and he was part of the decision making.

Whittingdale got what he wanted, there would be no story as to whether he'd used public money on official business and claimed on expenses for the hooker, flights, hotels etc.

She also (in a secret tape recording) said that Whittingdale wanted to keep their relationship, and for a while they should be careful, he made it clear to her that the fact she was a prostitute was obviously fine with him and that a "girls got to earn a living".

Well let's hope he debates that in the next Government debate on legalising prostitution, the HYPOCRITE.

## Twenty Eight

# NEW BEGINNINGS

When I first met William, it was all fun and games, a breath of fresh air, I'd been living in a cocoon with that Rudi all those Years back, I hadn't really lived like a young girl should, With Will it was wonderful, he taught me a lot how to not take life too seriously, I suppose that ok when you've got a trust fund in waiting. When we first met, he gave me the impression that he had the constitution of Keith Richards, and could handle any amount of alcohol, and although we all did coke, I just can't put my finger on when it escalated to crack. After he moved in with me at Redcliffe Square, Chelsea 1994, which I bought from the proceedings of a monumental amount of money made from Mr Twist the Billionaire I realised, he was having problems with his drink and drug use.

He once arrived home after yet another huge bender to tell me he'd spent the last 36 hours in a crack house. For the first six or seven hours he'd seen a man lying prone in the corner of the room, presumably asleep. Eventually the figure moved and got up and William recognised him as a chum from Eton!

I was amazed. "What did you talk about?" I asked.

"Natalie," he replied, "We were in a crack house. We didn't have time for chitchat."

William would get very intense and I was pregnant. I had stopped all drugs and alcohol, and didn't find it a problem to do so. My energy level was low and he was still up for the wild life, I wasn't. Arguments were more frequent, and I was exhausted from it all. On one occasion, William returned home after yet another long bender and became extremely aggressive and threatening towards me. I eventually felt so frightened I called the police. When the officers turned up, thanks to his accent and my skin-colour, they made assumptions and started talking to me as if I were the cause of all the trouble. William was the 'posh one' they even assumed that he owned the property, asking me If I had any where to go, until I swiftly corrected them. They were completely enamoured by him. Sir this, Sir that.

One of the officers went to have a look around the house and found a small amount of marijuana. "Is this yours?" he asked.

"No, I don't smoke marijuana, and besides I'm pregnant."

"If it is yours," he said, "I'll have to arrest you."

At that moment, William stepped in to admit it was his. They didn't arrest him, just gave him a caution. They were prepared to cart me – a pregnant woman – down to the police station but not his Lordship, even after he admitted it was his.

William had also left some foil he'd used to smoke crack in the bathroom. The officer came into the lounge and asked: "What do you think this is?"

"I don't know," I shot back, "What do you think?"

From the look on his face, I could tell I was only making trouble for myself, so I quickly changed tack.

"Oh, that? It's just a Kit Kat paper," "I was eating one in the bath earlier."

Off they went offering William a lift to where ever he wanted to go, well that's what you call Police service.

*

I went into labour while William was on a bender. I had my bag all packed and called up my friend Shel who was on her way. The Face restaurant (where I'd first laid eyes on William) was just across the road from the hospital. By sheer coincidence he was locking up the Restaurant, he saw me, came over and helped me with my suit case. What irony, I had met William at his restaurant, now pregnant and he's the one helping me with my luggage.

William showed up a few hours later, close to dawn, while I was still in labour, with a girl pal, I had met her in the past, another toff, and I knew they were just drug buddies.

I was having contractions and in severe pain, but was yet to be hooked up to an epidural, and they were in the en-suite bathroom snorting coke off the top of the cistern.

I wanted William there and so I thought, 'You know what? If he's happy, I just don't care what he gets up to.' At the same time I knew if he wasn't able to stop doing it now, at the birth of his son, then what hope was there?

I was just happy that Will had turned up, in whatever capacity.

I was in labour for 18 hours. Thank goodness Nicholas arrived as a perfectly healthy boy; he was my little miracle.

Another coincidence was that right in the opposite bed me to me in the maternity ward was Nicholas Coleridge' wife also having a baby, Christopher' brother. William had to navigate a mine field at visiting times as he didn't want anyone to know at the time, that he'd had a child.

William, on the other hand, was completely indifferent. He did nothing to rein in his behaviour and continued to smoked crack, away in one of the bedrooms or bathroom, in the house, I was busy being a mum, and he just didn't get it. Paraphernalia was left lying about the place.

"It won't do him any harm," he said, when I exploded at him.

The reason, William couldn't quite grasp that he was a father with responsibilities was because he just didn't know how. He was bought up in the stiff upper class kind of way, most of the Eton boys I've come across are very repressed, no wonder he rebelled, William's parents are now both deceased, but they at least left him a Multi- Million Trust Fund. They'd sent him off to a preparatory school as soon as they could, when he was just five years old.

William once told me story about when he lived on a farm and had his own pet sheep called Spinning Wheel, whom he loved dearly. One day he came home for dinner to find Spinning Wheel was nowhere to be seen. William asked where she was at supper and his mother replied that he was eating her.

William's parents died without wanting to see their grandson.

William kept bouncing in and out of rehab and both Chris and George thought he had become an arsehole. Out of everybody we knew, William had the best background, the brains, the looks - the whole package – anything George could have done (George used to be jealous of William), so could William, and more, William would have been a far better Politician than Cameron or Osborne could ever be, after all Politics runs through his veins after all his Grand Father Archibald Sinclair was a leading figure in British politics and his revival of the Liberal Party, helped bring them to where they are today….then Nick Clegg surfaced, to un -do all that had been achieved. Instead drink and drugs took a hold for a long period of his life.

I was so busy running the business and trying to look after Nicholas, who woke up every two hours, that it was only a matter of time before William pushed me over the edge. I finally kicked him out when Nicholas was five months old.

It was a relief to be on my own again. Although I'm enormously sociable, I love my own company. At a time in my life, I was most comfortable with my clients and my crowd, I lived in an unusual bubble, my whole life had been submerged in a world of vice and hedonism. I'm more in my comfort zone with the strange and wonderful types out there, normal… who wants normal that's boring.

Even with William gone, I was shattered trying to manage the escort business and Nicholas so, as I had no family in London to help, I hired a live-in nanny and relied on my wonderful Polish cleaner whom I'd known for years (she was originally the cleaner for Carol's flat in Holland Park and knew what I did, so was well used to cleaning up after my parties and domination sessions, although she drew a line at blood on the ceiling), who also helped look after Nicholas (she taught him Polish)..

Today - William has a great relationship with me and an even better one with our son, and more importantly he is drug and alcohol free.

# Twenty Nine

# GOING PUBLIC

By this time George Osborne had risen to the giddy heights of Shadow Chancellor and was managing David Cameron's campaign to become party leader. The newspapers were suddenly full of allegations that Cameron had taken cocaine as a young man – allegations that Cameron refused to answer. This got my attention with regard to what I knew about George. I was of great concern to George and those in the no knew that. He had been seen in private snorting cocaine on several occasions and more to the point by me, by my clients, and his associates. Was I going to expose him, apart from the fact that we had 'met up' in private and had engaged in sexual acts, if I went public it would have a great impact on my privacy, and William would be well and truly pissed off with me.

I watched the news intently, I was sitting on a story that WAS a matter of public interest, but should I tell what I knew. I first sought advice from Nigel my loyal client/friend, I discussed my thoughts with him, he was a Conservative and he didn't much like Osborne' ethics, and he didn't object. Nigel had known about George antics from the start although they had never met via me. So after a lot of consideration I called publicity guru Max Clifford to gauge interest. Eventually after I'd cancelled three appointments, I went down to Max' office in Mayfair. Max said my story was definitely in the public interest and, encouraged, I called William to discuss it with him.

"I'm thinking about doing something you won't like."

"Is it to do with George?"

William's response, caught me by surprise, It was clear to me that they all had already braced themselves.

"No, no, not George," I said, William was very intuitive, and he caught me by surprise.

I quickly dismissed his concerns, and mentioned nothing to him, of my plans.

The next day, Chris telephoned and asked if he could see me. I knew exactly what was on his mind, George was extremely close to Christopher, and he probably sent Christopher round to sound me out.

I had seen Chris a few months back, when he came over to collect some Charlie for him and George.

The last time I'd seen George in person was when I'd gone over to Christopher' home in Pembridge Villas, Notting Hill.

Chris and George had asked me to come round with some 'naughties', my son was with me, he was over 2 Years old by now, boy! How time had flown.

Once I arrived I gave the cocaine (2 grams) to Chris, he introduced me to a female sat on his Ikea dining table, (I had asked Chris where he'd bought the table from out of curiosity) and he had said Ikea. I did think to myself, all the millions Chris has and he buys Ikea, nothing wrong with Ikea stuff, I just thought his place would be less modern. Well he was always a bit thrifty.

I sat at the table with my son Nicholas beside me, while Chris and George was in the loo, obviously snorting a line. She stared back at me, observing me like I was some sort of alien. Who's this bitch, I thought in my head.

I'd been introduced to the lady, who later became his wife, Frances

The next day after Chris' call, he came round.

He stayed for a while and even came with me to Sainsbury's in Ladbroke Grove, where he kindly paid for my food shop. After paying for the shopping, he took out his Nectar Card – he still wanted those points! Mr Millionaire topping up the old nectar card, wonder how many he'd need for a bottle of Champers.

They were clearly worried because they thought I was about to say something.

"Look, whatever you think you're about to do," Chris said, "Don't do it."

But I went ahead and did it anyway. The media were already asking questions about both Cameron and Osborne's membership of the Bullingdon Club and debating whether they had taken drugs at university, so it made sense for me to make public what I knew.

Max originally planned to place my story with the News of the World but after the paper ran a negative story on Kerry Katona taking cocaine (Kerry was one of Max's best clients) he went to the Sunday Mirror who ran it on 16 October 2005, with the now infamous photograph of George and me at a party at my flat in 1994, with cocaine on the table.

Leading up to the story I was thoroughly interviewed and re interviewed by the journalist working for the Sunday Mirror, Susie Boniface, now more widely known under the pseudonym as 'Fleet Street Fox' Despite popular belief red tops work very hard to make sure that the story is completely true, and the Sunday Mirror was no exception. It wasn't just a case of believing me, they contacted many other potential witnesses and a lot of back ground work was undertaken. On the run up to the story Susie came by, today was the day I was to call Osborne and record our conversation. I called his secretary who said, she would get him to call me as soon as he was free, she said she would leave a message on his Blackberry, if he was unavailable to answer. Both I and Susie waited and waited...... and eventually my landline rang, "Natalie it's George" in his high pitched squeaky voice, we needed him to confess to taking cocaine. I told him that a journalist was asking me questions about his drug use, and what should I do, he had a panic in his voice and said, "If I didn't confirm anything then they wouldn't be able to say anything", "do you want me to lie about you taking cocaine George?" (I had to be very specific), and George Osborne proceeded to instruct me on how to deal with anyone asking questions about me and him. Susie had written down what I was to ask and under the stress of it all, I did a pretty good job. I didn't want him to suspect what I was up to, and miraculously he didn't. Osborne did more than confirm that I was telling the truth he had told me to lie about his cocaine use. I can only presume that after our conversation, he must have realised that he probably shouldn't have called me, but it was too late, I had caught him on the back foot.

On the Saturday before publication, a journalist from the News of the World appeared on my doorstep. Sarah Nuwar I'd met her before at Max' office when he had first considered going with the News of the World, I had given her the whole story in Max' office all about George' sex sessions with me, the drugs, parties the lot! But without my permission they couldn't run the story. She wanted to have a chat with me, I told her to go away, Susie had made it clear if any journalists turned up, I wasn't to open the door let alone speak to them. I said I had nothing to discuss with her. Without me giving them permission they couldn't run the story or so I thought. Sara was very persistent, and wouldn't budge. She had somehow got into the building and we were communicating through the door. She told me that the News of the world would be willing to pay me a huge amount of money for my story on George Osborne. I said that I was no longer interested in giving my story to any paper, and she should go away. I called Susie and she said to threaten her with the Police, that seemed to do the trick and she went away, but the drama had only just begun. Susie, got me a car, my head covered in case of a pap from N-O-W were lurking somewhere outside and I was whisked off to a hotel.

When my 'exclusive' story came out in the Sunday Mirror, the News of the World ran a front-page spoiler on the same day, accompanied by an editorial emphasising how George totally condemned drugs and that he was 'a young man who found himself caught up in this murky world'. I knew he was a lying hypocrite.

The following Monday-17/10/2005 in The Times - Andrew Pierce self-proclaimed 'Tory Boy' wrote - Ms Shackleton who Osborne knew as Nathalie (No! Tory Boy it's spelt Natalie) "In the first telephone call five months ago he listened but said little. When the ghost of his past returned about ten days ago he never returned her calls". Well! Thank goodness Susie Boniface a Journalist was with me when the liar Osborne CALLED ME, and it was never 5 months prior it was a couple of days on the run up to the Sunday Mirror story that Osborne called me. And then he went on to say ......Mr Osborne never fell for the trap. In the same article - A Conservative Central Office spokesman denied that Mr Osborne had a physical relationship with Ms Shackleton (me) "Nor has he ever taken drugs with her" Well as much as Osborne tried to spin and lie is way out of his murky past, all he did was dig a bigger hole.

The News of the World also distanced George from me: George was an innocent well-meaning young man while I was 'a cocaine-snorting call girl'. They also used an 'unnamed source' to further undermine my credibility.

I assumed I had a leak in my camp, - and someone at the News of the World had decided to try and kill the story. It worked. Tory MPs selected Cameron as leader of the Conservative Party the same month and this was made official in December 2005 after a ballot of Conservative Party members.

George's full statement in response to the Sunday Mirror article was:

"The allegations are completely untrue and dredging up a photo from when I was 22 years old is pretty desperate stuff."

This is merely part of a smear campaign to divert attention from the issues that matter in this leadership contest and I am confident people will not be distracted by this rubbish.

Twelve years ago a friend of mine went out with a woman called Natalie, (making out he barely knew me, the liar) and they had a child together.

I met them together occasionally in the autumn of 1993, and it soon became clear that my friend had started to use drugs.

He became more and more addicted and I saw his life fall apart.

With his other friends I tried to persuade him to seek treatment.

Eventually he did and after a long time in rehabilitation he has now recovered and put his life back together.

I am very proud of the battle he has fought and won.

That is, and always has been, the sum total of my connection with this woman.

It was a stark lesson to me at a young age of the destruction which drugs bring to so many people's lives.

Ever since then I have believed that tough, realistic policies to tackle the evil of drugs should be one of the top priorities of any government.

I now want to respect the privacy of my friend who is now happily recovered and working full-time abroad, and the privacy of his young child.

"For the sake of that child I think we should leave them alone."

William had far from recovered – and George did nothing to help him.

When George first got into Downing Street in 2010, he invited his closest friends to a cocktail party – except for William. George made every effort to prevent William - one of his very best friends - from coming. William was dreadfully hurt by this. William and many others could have and still could spill the beans on Osborne, but they've stayed quiet.

What is even more remarkable if not sinister is that Andy Coulson who was the Editor of the News of the World at the time they ran their front page story:

TOP TORY, COKE AND THE HOOKER, is that David Cameron (charlatan) on the advice of George Osborne then brought Andy Coulson right into the heart of Downing Street as their communications director. Osborne owed Coulson big time, Coulson had ran the story basically asking the reader to give Osborne the benefit of doubt.

When was there ever a time in History that the News of the World ran a sympathetic scandal on a Politician, Never to my recollection. And there had been no spy in my camp, Coulson and Co had been hacking my phone. I've seen a copy of the notes in Glenn Mulcaire's note book, given to me by the Police investigating the hacking scandal, ' Operation Weeting' with my name and people connected to me and Osborne. Osborne was hacked under the editorship of Coulson, but Osborne made no efforts to pursue the matter, stating that 'he had the Economy to run'. No back bone, a complete and utter liar, he had to keep Coulson sweet, why else would he employ him?, because Coulson knew the truth and tried to bury Osborne's debauched past.

He also said in his statement that he helped William clean up and he was now sober. This never happened. If anyone helped William, it was Chris, who did is bit to help.

George distanced himself from his friend and lied for the sake of his career. Meanwhile, the drug addict he didn't trust anymore now he was in power remained loyal to George, and stayed silent, even though George used William to take the media heat away.

When I was writing my book, as I reached the closing pages, I realised just how fortunate I am to have arrived at such a happy ending. Although I intend to keep my sexual adventures limited to pen and paper from now on, I still have my whip; never say never.

And a message to all the females out there; we all have a sell-by date, remember that in whatever path you choose!

And a BIG! shout out to all my followers on Twitter Xx

# Appendices

## I

# Is Your Partner Secretly into Domination?

1. Has your partner ever bought you high-heeled stiletto shoes or thigh high boots?

One client, whose wife didn't know that he was seeing me at the Gore Hotel in Queensgate, bought her some thigh high stiletto leather boots. He wanted his wife to look like a dominatrix, and even though she didn't know this – and although at first she thought it was odd - she now wears them all the time.

2. Has your husband ever referred to you as Mistress?

An obvious extension of this took place when I was shopping in the Kings Road Waitrose. A man leant across me to pick up something from the shelf and said: "Excuse me, Mistress."

3. Does he ever express desire to wear your underwear while making love to you? Has he ever worn them under his trousers when he goes to work?

JD (Lloyd's executive), my Norwegian banker and Nigel (one of my most longstanding clients) have all worn my underwear at work. JD used to send me texts telling me what he was wearing – usually my stockings and suspenders. This way, they feel like they're still my slave outside of my presence, plus the fact that they could be caught is thrilling for them – not that they want to get caught, of course.

4. Does he ever bring up the subject of corporal punishment? Does he seek your approval of the subject?

5. Does he likes being fingered in the ass while having sex, or likes you to use a dildo on him?

I didn't think that Rudi, my long-term boyfriend, was into domination, even though he used to like it when I put my fingers up there (up to three at a time). When we met up, years down the line, he wanted to be dominated – blindfolded and slapped. He said he always wanted me to do it but had been embarrassed to ask.

7. Does he come home with unexplained bruising on his body? (Especially his buttocks). If so, then he probably already has a Mistress (and probably had a particularly good session that night where he was in the moment and forgot he might have to explain the consequences of his punishment later on). I can't imagine it's easy to explain away – unless he's a footballer or gymnast.

8. Has he ever asked you to shave his genitals?

Lots of my slaves wanted me to do this. I asked one slave how he explained it to his wife. "I tell her I just want to be clean down there."

9. Does he admire or openly fancy strong, assertive, powerful women? Serena Williams is a good example. I love her strength, power and thick arms. What about Janet Street Porter? Grace Jones? Margaret Thatcher?

10. Does he likes having his nipples squeezed during sex?

Rudi liked this and it still didn't dawn me at the time that he might want to be a slave – almost every client gets to experience my nipple clamps.

11. Does he like to be blindfolded? And/or handcuffed?

This is very slave-like behaviour – he's literally in the dark, at your mercy.

12. Does he prefers you to choose his clothes?

A subtler sign of slave-like desires. My clients would sometimes give me some money to go shopping for them, for a tie for an event, for example. That way it's as if I still have some control over them while they're away.

13. Does he annoy you deliberately so that he can be berated and once you're angry does he want to have sex? (Or immediately after the row).

Clients have often said things to annoy me (occasionally even when they've taken me out for dinner, or at a party), knowing I'll remember it once we're in the midst of a session.

14. Did he go to Eton?

Chances are he's into domination.

# II

# A Ten-Step Beginner's Guide to Mistress-Slave Domination

- Both parties must be completely committed or it won't work, or be enjoyable. Put your desires before his – he doesn't count.

- Make sure that the day or evening for your fun will not be interrupted Continuity is essential – if you/he have to break role play to answer the door for the pizza delivery man it will ruin everything – you have to stay in the zone.

- Decide on your safe word so the slave can use it if he gets uncomfortable in any way. He must not misuse it – it can only be used if ABSOLUTELY necessary, as a last resort. If he misuses it, then the punishment is to stop the game altogether.

- Decide on the theme. Is he going to be your bitch for the day? Is he going to be a housekeeper, a naughty schoolboy, etc.?

- The Mistress shopping list: A cock ring, blindfold,

sterilised needles, rope, cat o'nine tails, whip, horsewhip, nipple clamps (ones with screws) handcuffs, dog collar, lead, ankle shackles, rubber pants.

- The Mistress Wardrobe: black, patent leather/plastic/rubber dress/skirt and bra. Fishnets or sheer black stockings, suspenders, the highest heels you can manage to walk in (all the better for him to suck on). Red or black basque.

- The Slave Wardrobe: Find out his shoe size and get some women's shoes for him, or order him to go and buy them himself (unless he'll be recognized). Many outlets specialise in larger size ladies' shoes. Shoes can be used in various ways during a session. For example, get him to parade around the room, if he stumbles then that's grounds for punishment.

- Be confident in your new persona. You're the bitch, Mistress, think of all times he pissed you off and you said nothing. If he steps out of line then slap or cane him to your heart's content but whatever you do, do not slip in and out of character. Let him know you are the real deal.

- The slave must not suggest anything – you do not need his blessing for anything you want to do.

- Use role-play, it's a useful way of keeping you both in character. For example, sit him on a chair. Handcuff his hands behind the chair and blindfold him. Then sit on him straddling his legs and demand he give you five reasons why he deserves you. If you don't like any of the answers, then squeeze his nipples, increasing pain accordingly. Command him to pleasure your nipples with his tongue. Threaten him with the paddle. Gently slap his face, building up pain. You can also do this in bed if you prefer. He has to satisfy you, any which play you please.

# III

# Bitch For the Day Role Play

In this role play you will need either a cane or the cat o'nine tails. I prefer the cane, as it allows for a precise aim, whereas the cat o'nine sometimes has a mind of its own (it's a good idea to practise with the nine on your own for a bit, then impress him with your expertise). If you're punishing his cock, then the cane is better. The cat is great for the buttocks – marks will appear immediately but will only last beyond that night if you're using a lot of strength.

In the morning when he's going to work, for example, make him wear your knickers and hold-ups underneath his trousers (if you give him suspenders and he crosses legs people will see the clips). This way he will spend the day profoundly aware of what is waiting for him once he gets home - don't be surprised if he comes home earlier than usual. If that happens (or if he's silly enough to be late), then make sure you punish him for it during the session.

You will have already bought him some shoes in his size. Lay out the dog collar, lead, shoes, wig and dildo on the floor. Be ready in your mistress attire. When he arrives, order him to take off everything except his knickers and stockings. Have your reddest lippy at hand and tell him to put it on – compliment him as you see fit, tell him what a perfect little whore he is. Then you're ready.

If he tries to be giggly or gives you a sly smile, suggesting it's just a game, then punish him. This is serious. It can happen sometimes but if he's into it straight away and seems to be the perfect slave, then he's probably done it before.

Whatever punishment you give him, you are in control - resist the urge to check if he's ok. He's a big boy and he's got the safe word if he can't handle what you're dishing out to him.

Have him parade himself around the room, walking or crawling in his new persona. When you've had enough of that spread your legs and let him pleasure your pussy with his mouth – tell him what you want and how you want it – order him to run his tongue slowly round the outside of your vagina. Remember, you're also experiencing something new, so take your time and enjoy it.

You should have the cane in your hands and beat him if he's not sucking or licking to your requirements.

Put some honey on your high heels (maybe with a dash of tabasco because we don't want him to feel comfortable) and order him to slowly lick them. Dip your heel into his mouth and get him to suck it slowly – reach for the cane out if he tries to stop or isn't doing it well enough. Tell him that he is privileged to serve you as you stand over him with your heel in his mouth. If he still isn't up to scratch then threaten him by telling him you'll find a new slave – that always winds them up.

Printed in Great Britain
by Amazon.co.uk, Ltd.,
Marston Gate.